THE COMMON SENSE LIFE:

TALES FROM A LONG AGO FOREST

DONALD R. REPSHER

~WITH~

ROBERT "RED HAWK" RUTH
PHILIP GRAYWOLF
CHUCK "GENTLE MOON" DEMUND
CAROL KUHN

ILLUSTRATIONS BY PAMELA REPSHER

Copyright ©2015 by Donald R. Repsher. All rights reserved. No part of this publication may be reproduced, stored in a retrieval system or transmitted in any form or by any means electronic, mechanical, photocopying, recording, or otherwise, except in the case of brief quotations embodied in critical articles or reviews, without the prior written permission of the author.

Quotations in this book, unless otherwise noted, are taken from historical documents believed to be in the Public Domain, or Lenape oral tradition.

ISBN: 0-9851833-4-9
ISBN-13: 978-0-9851833-4-9

I send greetings from the Lenape Nation. Much has been written about my people over the last three centuries. Very few have taken the time to talk to us and get to know us. Donald Repsher is one of those who approached us with a good heart. He has sat at our councils and enjoyed our fireside chats. Our people have bestowed on him the term "Uncle." In our culture that is one of the highest honors. The Lenape Nation thanks our brother for sharing the culture and history of our people.

    In the Lenape Spirit,
        Chief Bob Red Hawk

"In the woods I am blessed."
    – Ludwig von Beethoven to his nephew

TABLE OF CONTENTS

	Preface	5
	Forward: What is Spirituality?	13
1	Before the Beginning	17
2	Wisdom From the Almost-Forgotten	21
3	One or the Other – or Both/And Plus?	25
4	Discretion and Valor	29
5	Columbus and the Most Important Journey	33
6	Verrazano: He Didn't Jump to Conclusions	37
7	Natives Discover Henry Hudson	41
8	Living on the Back of a Giant Turtle	45
9	The Forest People	49
10	Wild Turkey People	53
11	The People Who Knew Wolves	57
12	Who Owns What?	61
13	It's So Frustrating!	65
14	Wisdom Within Rocks	69
15	A Chain of Friendship	73
16	Vision for Now and Always	77
17	Tamanend and a Civil Civilization	81
18	Tamanend: America's Patron Saint	85
19	Imagine!	89
20	Lingering a Little Longer	93
21	More Time With Eyewitnesses	97
22	Promises	101
23	The Smiles of Greed	105
24	Respect	109
25	Egotism – and Compassion	113
26	Gratitude	117
27	When Crisis Comes	121
28	Alliance of the Waters	125
29	Shingas Weeps	129
30	Courage	133
31	The Silent Years	137
	And Now to Begin	143
	Biographical Information	145
	Bibliography	149

PREFACE

This is not a history book, but the stories herein do provide glimpses into history whose lessons, if learned, can contribute toward a civil civilization as well as a genuinely worthwhile human life. Along with a few traditional stories, we will travel across a bridge between history and philosophy in a vehicle steered by wisdom and fueled by spirituality found within the words "living with a good heart."

Think of wisdom as the steering wheel navigating us in the right direction along a new highway with many possible interchanges. Think of spirituality as the fuel keeping us moving, and without which we would be going nowhere.

I have relied heavily upon old, almost-forgotten documents. These documents provide clues to help us attempt something seldom—if ever—done before: travel to a village of long-ago ancestors and look into the hearts of human beings who lived and learned about the purpose of human life many, many long years ago. The documents to which we will refer are like maps that need to be frequently updated. Capitalization, spelling, punctuation, and paragraphing have changed since these documents were written. They have been modernized to make them more readable. The words remain as they were. They are like a landscape that remains the same while plant life changes with the seasons.

Possibly from the dawn of their existence the Lenape ancestors were friendly, hospitable, unpretentious, and peaceable. One fascinating observation is that while there is plentiful archaeological evidence of violent wars in Europe and elsewhere, archaeologists have detected no signs of walled villages in Lenape-hocking (the homeland of the Lenape). The absence of protective walls is indicative of peaceful pursuits.

But there *is* evidence of cultural changes. Does this mean that people were being displaced by violence, or were the people open to new ideas from outside as well as from within their own ranks? Cultural changes do not require violence and war. We ourselves were witnesses to non-violent cultural changes. Automobiles replaced horses. Airplanes entered the sky. Computers replaced typewriters. People from other places in the world arrived and made their own contributions.

For over two hundred fifty years the best of their ancient heritage has been hidden like seeds in the soil, waiting to germinate. Now, in the twenty-first century, present-day descendants in Pennsylvania are recovering and honoring traditions that have been carefully kept within the privacy of individual families. We can return to where we live now, enriched in mind and heart by our visit with people who lived on the other side of the mountain of time.

The documents from colonial Pennsylvania I have read tell me something very different from my memories of public school and the movies. Although many settlers lived in villages and towns, farmhouses were far apart and not protectively clustered together. If danger from Indians had been a problem why did so many pioneers choose to live in a wide-open landscape? Indians shared their crops and their knowledge of hunting with their white neighbors. People of European ancestry could travel mile after mile along ancient Indian trails through mountains and forests without fear of being assaulted. Many of those ancient trails have become the highways and country roads of today.

It is my hope that the following chapters will encourage Lenape descendants to appreciate and take pride in the wisdom and spirituality fostered by the best of their ancestors. It is also my hope that some of us who are not genetically related will begin to feel a kinship with our Native predecessors in America. Not that we should become "wannabee" Indians! Instead we should acknowledge that America's history did not begin with Columbus but had a long life of thousands of years before he came on the scene. And more than that: we can begin to recognize and learn from the wisdom those people of long ago accumulated over the passage of time.

The word Lenape (pronounced "Le-NAH-pay") means "people." It's unpretentious, perhaps identifying them simply as human beings. A word that is sometimes attached to it, "Lenni," means "original people." It may infer that some of those who lived in Lenape-hocking came from elsewhere and became part of the people who were already there. The name is symbolic of the kind of people they were, continually welcoming and assimilating newcomers and thereby creating through thousands of years the original "melting-pot" of civilization on the North American continent. A more specific name is "Delawares," which is an English term for the river that runs through their ancient homeland and a reminder of the place of origin for the people who are now living elsewhere.

The story of the Lenape points to a long, complex tradition of hospitality and assimilation in Lenape-hocking, which includes southeastern New York State, eastern Pennsylvania, New Jersey, and Delaware. The Lenape were held in high regard by many other Indian nations. They were referred to as "grandfathers," a term of respect implying not only their ancient status but their wisdom and spirituality. The Lenape referred to other Indian nations as "cousins," "uncles," "nephews," "brothers." "We are all related" also refers to trees, animals of the forests, in fact everything in the Great Spirit's creation. Nothing in scientific knowledge disputes this ancient insight. In one way or another we are indeed all related. We depend upon the oxygen that plants and trees convert from the carbon dioxide we breathe out. Without this mutual relationship, life as we know it could not be sustained.

Other American Indians also have profound contributions to make. There is much to learn from all of them. I cannot include everyone in the colorful variety of traditions that once made this a culturally diverse continent. Instead I have chosen to limit myself to those I know. All deserve to have their own profound wisdom and spirituality respected.

It is important to recognize that no one needs to depart from her or his own religious beliefs in order to benefit from the insight and experiences of those who lived in Lenape-hocking. Truth is universal. I agree with my Lenape friends that true religion is not marked by creeds but by a good heart. No one can have a true religion, no matter what the creed or outward form, without being good-hearted. Living without a good heart distorts the soul of any religious doctrine.

Appreciation

I am grateful to Chiefs Bob Red Hawk and Waktame (Philip Greywolf), "Chuck" Gentle Moon DeMund, clan mother Carol Kuhn, and others for their patience, kindness, and assistance; and to all my Lenape friends for being who they are. I also want to thank my wife Pamela for her faithful encouragement as well as her illustrations throughout this book. Ed and Millie Henning have been a great help in proof-reading. Special thanks to my editor and publisher, David Repsher, for his great help in getting rid of flaws and improving the flow of the text. Our children, their spouses, and our grandchildren are appreciated for being the fine persons they are. I am thankful for the trust that my deceased parents gave to me. The friendship of all my relatives and friends is cherished.

Nor can I forget my pastor of many years ago, Lester Updegrove, who took me aside when I was entering college and gave me this advice which I now pass along:

"You will encounter new ideas. Never be afraid to take time to look at them and evaluate them carefully. If any new idea fits you better than what you've had previously, don't be afraid to accept it. If it isn't better for you, leave it."

This advice has provided a lifetime of freedom to think and explore. I'm reminded that the earth was created with variety and color, freeing life from the monotony of being confined into one mold.

And now...

We begin with a Lenape definition of spirituality which can be summed up in five words: "Living with a good heart." This is followed by a Lenape tradition about the origins of this world. Next we will examine several glimpses into early European explorations of the eastern North American continent, which serves as a preview into what the Lenape and other indigenous people would encounter from newcomers whose origins were far across the wide expanse of water. Then we will focus specifically upon the Lenape who lived within Lenape-hocking and were respectfully acknowledged by many of their neighboring nations as "grandfathers."

Each brief chapter can be read, if you wish, as a personal examination of the present—a daily devotional reading, perhaps. You can create your own prayer at the end of each chapter. Or you can simply read along as you would any other book.

FORWARD

What is spirituality?
Phillip Graywolf (Wipunkwteme)

The life of a Spiritual Warrior is challenging and rewarding. One of its basic challenges is to engage life fully. To make full use of both beauty and challenges in order to gain wisdom and find our true selves. To learn to love, trust, and walk in beauty. To be in balance and harmony and walk a fearless life.

With prayer we find connections that are absolute, whole, total, clean, full, correct, better, aimed, complete, best, good, excellent, unbounded, clear, even, real, plain, certain, pure, fair, genuine, sincere in all things.

To begin with, this means we must be willing to observe. We must be willing to look at the obvious aspects of our life. We must be willing to look deeper below the surfaces of life. And we must be willing to do so without denial or acting like victims.

We work to become aware of the influences of our past and to clear them, as well as to face new experiences with openness, responsibility, and curiosity. Our primary questions, when faced with either an opportunity or a challenge, are these: "What is the lesson here? How can I make the best of this to learn for myself and serve all my relations?"

Once we are truly willing to see, then we are confronted with many choices. How do I make the best use of the particular talent I've been given? Do I want to do the hard work required to clear up an old unworkable pattern? Am I willing to let it continue to drain my spiritual power away? How can I learn well the lessons that have called to me?

Choosing to work on it is the best way to begin.

Aware that we learn from each and every experience, the Spiritual Warrior is willing to choose. Whatever we choose will lead to new experiences and give feedback upon which to base our next choice. This means the Spiritual Warrior, once perceiving a choice, will not only choose—but act!

Spiritual growth is taking responsibility for life as it unfolds day to day. It is learning to love without attaching the strings of expectation. It means establishing intimate communications with trustworthy others. It means treasuring self-esteem for the special gift it is. It means acting with the integrity that flows from highly-developed principles.

Spiritual growth means discovering the abundance of bright green grass on one's own side of the fence. It means mastering the discouraging fears of unknown tomorrows. It means planning for the future without living in it. It means new dreams from lessons learned.

Spiritual growth means moving beyond the quest for material possessions. It means pursuing aspirations with fewer disruptions to our well-being. It means creating a more positive and balanced existence every day. It means seeking a generous measure of peace and contentment wherever we may be and in whatever is going on. It means treating each unique moment as a cherished memory to come. It means lifting someone else's spirits when pain enters that person's world. It means trading smugness and complacency for enthusiasm and innovation.

Spiritual growth means feeding the Spirit with love, play, compassion, hope, and prayers. It means working with others without seeking power over them. It means understanding the lack of true perfection in all of us. It means accepting ourselves for who we are this very instant!

Spiritual growth means overcoming the desire to live another person's life by learning to honor their truths.

Spiritual growth means knowing we'll be much wiser where we're going than where we've been. It means teaching what we know with humility as our own awareness expands. It means eliminating the arrogance that knowledge occasionally brings. It means seeing the fullness of life rather than too much emptiness.

Spiritual growth means welcoming the honest input of friends or perceived foe. It means spending time with ourselves and our Creator. It means moving diligently toward the light of knowingness. It means releasing whatever hold guilt has on our life. It means validating all feelings and experiences as real. It means forgiving ourselves and others for being human.

Spiritual growth means serving humankind in our own special way. Spiritual growth means living gratefully within our means.

CHAPTER 1

BEFORE THE BEGINNING

Bob Red Hawk says: "If you want to know about the Lenape people, about our culture, about our history, you can't just start in the middle. You must go back. The elders always said that if you want to know the original intent the Creator had for our people, if you really want to know who we are, don't look at a hundred years ago, and don't look at five hundred years ago. Instead, go back to the beginning because that's who we are today. What happened in the beginning shaped who we are today."

Documents show the Lenape were always capable of abstract thinking: to understand the meaning of something it is necessary to think beneath the surface. People of wisdom among the Lenape were such profound thinkers their thoughts went beyond the beginning of time to *before* the beginning.

And now, as almost all civilizations tell their earliest stories through poetry, here is a story as told to me by Chief Bob Red Hawk:

Before the beginning there was nothing but darkness
But in the darkness there lived a Spirit
In the darkness Spirit just existed
And in the darkness Spirit fell asleep
In darkness, and in sleep, Spirit dreamed

In the dream, Spirit saw the earth
In darkness and in the dream, Spirit saw the mountains
The waterfalls
Rivers and lakes
Birds flying in the air
Deer walking softly in the forests
Spirit saw people
Spirit heard ceremonies
Spirit heard the drum

And to this day, before we begin to do anything
Before we get up in the morning
We think

In our heart we see the earth
We see the mountains
In our heart we see waterfalls and rivers and lakes
Birds flying in the air
And deer walking softly in the forests
In our heart we see people
And hear ceremonies
And hear the drum

In our heart we sing the songs
And we think
We are children of the Creator
We have the ability to think
And dream of what can be

Every new day begins with gratitude and a vision of what can be just as Creator, the Great Spirit, did before the beginning of time. What an excellent way to live before each day even begins!

Before leaping into busyness there is thoughtfulness. Perhaps there will be joy; perhaps there will be pain, or perhaps a mingling of both. There is also a vision of something valuable the day can bring to both one's self and to others.

If there is no dream—no vision at all—how can there be hope? A meaningful life—any meaningful enterprise—requires a vision. Only with a vision of what can be is there the possibility of bringing light from darkness, which is one of the great insights of the Lenape way: without a vision of what *can be* there is little worthwhile that is likely *to be*.

CHAPTER 2

WISDOM FROM THE ALMOST-FORGOTTEN

Dare we even try to imagine the cultural and spiritual values which enabled the "Original People" (principally located in present-day eastern Pennsylvania, New Jersey, and parts of Delaware) to live with themselves, their relatives, their neighbors, strangers, and their environment thousands of years ago?

Caves and shelters where families crowded beneath overhanging rocky ledges provided protection from rain and snow. Agriculture was still unknown in any part of the world, so food was obtained by hunting and gathering the plentiful supplies of animals, fruits and fish.

Life survived by making sacrifices. That was the nature of reality. It was evident everywhere. Plants and trees died, decayed, and nourished new life. Small animals fed larger animals. Sacrifices are not pleasant, but necessary for preserving the planet and perpetuating life itself.

Likewise, human life required making sacrifices. Adults could not simply feed themselves, it was necessary to share food with children. The best way to assure a future for one's self was to learn at an early age the importance of doing without some things, at least for awhile, and sharing with others. Sacrifice was the unchangeable law of nature. The ancestors were close observers of nature and sacrifice, and their careful observations taught them the wisdom of an essential lesson in life: without sacrifice there is no future.

The twentieth century ushered in the impression that sacrifice is something to be avoided. Nature came to be looked upon as "blood-red in tooth and claw." People began to wonder why the Deity could be so cruel as to allow sacrifice. It became easy to forget even light is devoured by darkness, and in turn darkness is devoured by light. Perhaps in some other universe there is never any need for making sacrifices, but not in this universe, this world, or in this life. The spirit of people who try to live without making sacrifices will eventually wither and perish upon the altar of greed.

The people who lived here thousands of years ago, like humans everywhere, made mistakes. Some tried to break the rules. But life in small villages tended to make privacy difficult. Cultural standards of conduct were substantial. The silent treatment of being ignored by one's neighbors was often punishment enough, but to be forever banished for breaking those standards was severe.

Life ebbed and flowed. The people laughed and cried. They worried. They believed. They had arguments. They learned that sometimes forgiveness is better than contaminating their spirit with self-destructive seeds of anger. Yes, we can be sure they hated, because some disputes led to bloodshed. But they also loved. They made a life for themselves within their environment not by trying to conquer it but by getting along with it.

There was memory as well as sacrifice. The wisdom of what was good for survival not only passed from one person to another, but from one generation to another. Significant stories providing insight were passed on to following generations where each person was expected to draw his or her own conclusions about that insight.

The forests themselves may have encouraged intellectual freedom. Heavy tree growth darkened the forests and kept undergrowth from completely blocking Indian trails, which are evidence of extensive travel. Who knows how many hundreds or thousands of years ago those trails were first made and used? Being alone in the woods with scarcely any sunlight coming through the trees, even on a well-marked trail, can foster fear and awe, but can also encourage solitary thinking, which then can promote individualism. Individualism resists autocracy and allows the freedom to make personal choices. And, unless people think for themselves, there will be those who thrive on tyranny.

Whatever their distant origins, individualism, respect for personal choices, and equality are traditional marks of Lenape culture. Repeated historical references to Lenape chiefs as "kings" are mistakes made by those bred in European customs. They could not imagine any other kind of government. Yes, all Lenape villages had their own chief, but decisions were made in council, not by some kind of royal authority. A chief who made too many decisions without consulting the village council could easily be dismissed. The "original people" were among the world's first true democracies.

"Lenape" simply means "people." Among other things, it's a humble word. It's not at all pretentious. If we could transport ourselves back thousands of years we might ask them "By what name are you known?" The answer would likely be "People." Just "People." The word included everything. We're all related. There are four-legged people in the forests. Trees were considered one-legged people. Two-legged people felt a profoundly personal relationship with the earth.

We *are* all related. Everything on earth should be respected. Everything has a spiritual nature and is part of the People.

We can easily forget this in our world of concrete, steel, macadam, and fantastic technology. But if we recognize the insights the almost-forgotten people would have needed to survive we might understand the roots of wisdom and spirituality. Consider them carefully. Willingness to make sacrifices. Humility instead of arrogance. A sense of relationship with all the earth. This is the Lenape way. This is the way of genuine people.

The ancient ones were not lacking in wisdom or spirituality. They knew the value of living with a good heart. Do not forget. These values contained within the human spirit are essential for human well-being and human survival in every century.

CHAPTER 3

ONE OR THE OTHER OR BOTH/AND PLUS?

I have a few all-time favorite cartoons from the *Saturday Review* which was published by Norman Cousins in the 1950s when there was controversy over whether environment or heredity was more important. In one cartoon, a little boy brings home his school report, which is obviously not a good one judging by the way the boy's father is glowering. "Tell me, Father," asks the boy, "which is most responsible for my terrible school report: heredity or environment?" I can imagine the father coming close to having a melt-down.

"Chuck" Gentle Moon, one of my Lenape friends, has, in my opinion, a good answer. For the Lenape, it is neither heredity nor environment, it is both—plus the personal choices made during a lifetime.

Heredity was an important influence in the life of all people throughout the ancient world. Parents needed to be strong to survive. Their children either inherited physical strength or, if they were too sickly and weak, perished.

A person's environment was also substantial. The environment of a small village, with grandparents and other elders always nearby, as well as the close proximity of neighbors, exercised social control and helped keep growing children from doing rash and foolish things.

Personal choices were consequential, as my Lenape friend suggests. Personal choices build a life, one choice upon another. As a clan mother explained to me, for example, her Lenape grandmother felt Christian teachings encouraged last-minute repentance with entrance into Heaven after an entire lifetime of wasteful choices. The grandmother was convinced this diminished the importance of living throughout one's life with good personal choices.

It was by personal choice that a young Lenape man and a girl fell in love and were married. Tradition required the girl to prove her cooking ability by preparing a meal that would bring honor to her husband-to-be. The young man was required to go into the woods and not return until he could bring meat for his future bride to cook. By contrast, marriages among the upper classes in Europe were arranged, and if a person fell in love with someone beneath his or her social status the prospect of marriage was almost hopeless. Personal choice was belittled.

In Lenape-hocking, personal choice could allow an unhappy wife to end her marriage with an intolerable husband. While she might discuss the problems with friends or family, it was the Lenape wife alone who made the decision. Then, it was only necessary for her to collect her husband's meager possessions and put them outside the wigwam. When the husband returned, tradition required him to quietly pick up his possessions and leave. Compare this to European culture where a wife was her husband's possession, and she had very little protection from being mistreated. The expression "Rule of thumb" came from Europe, and dictated that no husband could beat his wife with a stick larger in diameter than his thumb.

Grandmothers in Lenape-hocking took care of children while mothers worked in the vegetable gardens. There were no orphanages or foster homes. Those who lost parents and grandparents became the responsibility of their mother's female relatives and were not removed from friends they knew.

The Lenape were not bound by hereditary "rights," as were Europeans. Clan mothers chose the village chief based on his merit. Chiefs were servants of the people: responsible for leading ceremonies, distributing food to all (beginning with the elders), and other duties concerning the people's welfare. In time of war, a war-chief known for his ability was then selected from among the villages.

Personal privileges meant personal responsibilities. Each person was expected to spend time coming to a wise decision best suited for that person and not in conflict with village traditions. Keeping a balance was emphasized.

Some traditional Lenape went on a vision quest and continue to do so today. Alone both day and night, with fasting and prayer, the seeker waited until a vision came and revealed what course should be taken.

"It was very eerie out on the mountain all alone throughout the long, long nights," says Bob Red Hawk. "The vision would come sooner if physical labor was also involved." This included gathering rocks and making a mound or pillar.

It was not expected that everyone should fit into the same mold. Quite the contrary, the Lenape recognized that just as a forest is filled with a variety of plant and animal life, so human communities should anticipate a variety of personalities.

Heredity. Environment. Personal choices. All of them are connected. None can exist without the others. And privileges cannot be separated from responsibilities.

CHAPTER 4

DISCRETION AND VALOR

Discretion and valor: they were already second nature to native people at the time of the first encounter with Europeans possibly a thousand years ago.

We cannot generalize and think all natives were alike. The people of Lenape-hocking may have been very different from the Skraelings (Norse word meaning "little men") who met Karlsefni the Norseman, who ventured even further than the better-known Leif Ericson. His story was carried by word of mouth for three hundred years before it was written by Hauk Erklendsson about 1300 A.D. and translated by A. M. Reeves in 1890. Albert Bushnell Hart included this document in the first volume of his *American History Told by Contemporaries.*

With three ships, 160 men, and several women, Karlsefni sailed beyond the farthest Norse settlements and landed briefly at a place of large flat rocks and many arctic foxes. Sailing on, they discovered an island with many bears. The mainland was heavily forested. The narrative continues that sailing southward "for a long time" they came upon a cape where they saw part of a shipwreck. Some unknown Europeans had been there before them!

They landed soon afterward and some people were sent to explore inland. They later returned having seen no one, but one of the explorers carried a bunch of grapes, and another an ear of wheat. Human habitation was apparent. But where were the people?

Karlsefni sailed on, finally reaching an island surrounded by strong currents, but he decided to winter on the mainland which had mountains.

The narrative then informs us that some in the expedition decided in late spring to sail northward "in search of Vineland." Karlsefni and his group, however, continued southward, again "for a long time." Spring became summer, then autumn. At last they came to a river which "flowed down from the land into a lake and so into the sea." Sandbars made it impossible to enter the river except at high tide. After finally sailing into the river, "They found self-sown wheat-fields." Grapevines were also present. Every brook was full of fish, and the forest held a great variety of animals. They decided to spend the winter there. They built huts above the lake and allowed their livestock to wander freely.

One morning, a month after landing, they saw canoes approaching. These were not dugout logs like those used in the distant northland, these were canoes covered with animal skins. "They were swarthy men, and ill looking," the Norse document states. "The hair of their heads was ugly. They had great eyes, and were broad of cheek." They came ashore and silently stared at the Norsemen "for a long time." Then they returned to their boats and rowed away southward "around the point." Throughout the winter "no snow came there" and their livestock grazed freely.

A large contingent of "skin-canoes" arrived the next spring, and trading began by exchanging "peltries and quite gray skins" for red-cloth. Despite several requests from the Skraelings, Karlsefni refused to trade away any swords or spears. The trading was suddenly interrupted when a bull belonging to Karlsefni's people rushed bellowing loudly from the woods. The startled Skraelings ran to their canoes and rowed quickly away.

Three weeks passed. Then the narrative reports "a great multitude of Skraeling boats was discovered approaching from the south." The Skraelings were howling loudly, and as soon as their canoes landed, they sprang to the ground. A battle ensued. The Natives used war-slings and punctuated the air with missiles. Then the narrative informs us that something peculiar occurred.

> *The Skraelings raised upon a pole a great ball-shaped body, almost the size of a sheep's belly, and nearly black in colour, and this they hurled from the pole up on the land above Karlsefni's followers, and it made a frightful noise where it fell.*

With the Skraelings at their heels, the Norsemen fled until they reached "jutting crags" and "offered a stout resistance." Freydis, one of their women, could not keep up and ran into the woods where she stumbled upon a dead Norseman whose skull had been cleft by a flat stone. She gripped his sword. As the Natives approached her she beat the sword upon her breast and dared them to fight. They hurriedly retreated, leaped into their boats, and rowed away.

Now aware of the danger, the Norsemen loaded their ships and sailed away northward, never to return.

There are several important clues here that may also characterize native people who lived in far-off Lenape-hocking. One was the natives' discretion. They carefully observed the Norsemen's peculiar ships coming slowly toward their land. Not knowing what dangers this might pose, what other conclusion can we draw than the entire native population disappeared into the hills to see what kind of people these strangers were? That is discretion.

Did the Natives believe the Norsemen's bull to be a terrifying weapon? Did they spend the next three weeks contacting their allies along the coast to ensure they would have enough men to defeat the strangers? Again, this reveals their discretion as only *then* did they exhibit their valor.

Elsewhere, references to "Original People" and other tribes reveal discretion—as well as valor—as wide-spread characteristics. Perhaps we can learn some wisdom for living in the twenty-first century: It is wise to give discretion priority over valor. An old adage says it well: Look carefully before you leap

CHAPTER 5

COLUMBUS AND THE MOST IMPORTANT JOURNEY

It's amazing how someone can know so much and understand so little.

Christopher Columbus had grown up in the Church. His journey, with three ships under his command, was blessed by the Pope and financed by the king and queen of Spain. He believed the world is round and so did others. His journal has apparently been lost, but it was abridged by Las Casa. His abridgment was translated in 1880 by H. L. Thomas and included in Hart's *American History told by Contemporaries*. What happened to the good-hearted natives Columbus met is a prelude to what followed 350 years later.

By Thursday, October 11, 1492, discouragement was growing on board his three ships. Rebellion was in the air. Then they saw signs of land: a reed, a stick, pieces of grass, a small board. "In view of such signs," Las Casa wrote, "they breathed more freely and grew cheerful." They reached an island in the Caribbean Sea and the story continues:

> *The Admiral called the two captains and the rest who had come on shore, and Rodrigo Descovedo, the Notary of all the fleet, and Rodrigo Sanchez de Segovia, and he called them as witnesses to certify that he in the presence of them all was taking ... said island for the King and Queen his masters....*
>
> *Soon after a large crowd of natives congregated there. What follows are the Admiral's own words.... 'In order to win the friendship and affection of that people, and because I am convinced that their conversion to our Holy Faith would be better promoted through love than through force, I presented them with red caps and some strings of glass beads which they placed around their necks, and with other trifles of insignificant worth that delighted them and by which we have got a wonderful hold on their affections....*
>
> *They are of good size, good demeanor, and well formed. I saw some with scars on their bodies, and to my signs asking them what these meant, they answered in the same manner, that people from neighboring islands wanted to capture them, and they had defended themselves.... They must be good servants and very intelligent, because I saw that they repeat very quickly what I told them, and it is my conviction that they would easily become Christians, for they seem not to have any sect. If it please our Lord, I will take six of them to your Highnesses on my departure, that they may learn to speak.'*

Columbus never came near Lenape-hocking. But the tragedy of what happened to the people he met would happen again and again throughout the Western Hemisphere, including Lenape-hocking. Death followed the white man's footsteps.

The first thing Columbus did was to take possession of the land for a European monarchy. In Native spirituality the land, the water, and the air belong to the Great Spirit who oversees all. In Biblical spirituality the same insight is clearly stated: "The earth is the Lord's and all that is in it" (Psalm 24:1, New Revised Standard Version). But Columbus acted as if the natives' land could ethically be taken away from them and given to a far-off monarchy. He understood so little.

Columbus, at first, thought of winning the friendship of the people not by force but by love, which is commendable. But he betrayed his good intentions by assuming he held a monopoly on spirituality. He confused religion with spirituality, and thought the natives had neither. He exhibited no inclination to learn what they held in their hearts. This attitude would persist for centuries to come.

He tried to impress the natives with glittering trifles. He knew their cheap value, the natives didn't. They were amazed at the sparkling pieces of glass they received. Columbus seized the advantage. Questionable business deals are like this. Some dealers welcome unsuspecting, trusting customers and do not consider the value of honesty and integrity or long-term consequences when profit instead of honor becomes the ultimate goal.

Columbus thought natives were objects for exploitation, and he thought his deity approved: "If it please our Lord I will take six of them...." He took these human beings from their homes, their families, and their people, as if he owned them; allowing self-interest to take the place of humane responsibilities.

Lastly, Columbus was convinced that unless the people he encountered spoke his language and shared his ideas and his religion, they were ignorant.

In short, Christopher Columbus was blind to his own faults and failed to see beyond his own nose. It's a common human characteristic, which spelled doom for friendly, hospitable, and trusting natives. He betrayed their kindness. Throughout history this same self-deceit has brought disaster to many, including disasters that came to the people who lived for thousands and thousands of years in Lenape-hocking.

Remember the tragedy of Christopher Columbus's own soul. He knew so much but understood so little. He not only failed to know where he was, he failed to travel the most important journey of all—that which fosters respect for others, reaches deep into human hearts, and touches them with a humane spirit.

Think about it. For what purpose were we given the gift of life here on earth? Self-interest above all else, or a balance between self-interest and concern for the quality of life around us?

CHAPTER 6

VERAZZANO: HE DIDN'T JUMP TO CONCLUSIONS

Captain John Verrazano was born and raised in Florence, Italy, but it was King Francis I of France who funded his voyage of exploration along the coast of America.

Verrazano sailed in 1524, thirty-two years after Columbus's well-known journey. The report he wrote for King Francis was translated in 1860 by Joseph G. Cogswell. In this document Verrazano shows some of the self-discipline that often kept him from jumping to mistaken conclusions. He did not, like Columbus, speculate about going around the world and finding Asia.

He wrote: "We reached a new country which had never been seen by anyone either in ancient or modern times." Now, at this point he *did* jump to a mistaken conclusion, because he did not know about the Norsemen's explorations five hundred years before. He forgot that the people he saw were living proof that the land had already been discovered by countless explorers. No one is perfect. It helps to be somewhat tentative about most conclusions we make because they may be based on insufficient knowledge.

Week after week Verrazano and his shipmates followed the coastline south. At last he brought his ship close to land, anchoring before reaching dangerous shoals, and then went the rest of the way by boat. Astonished inhabitants greeted him. "The complexion of these people is black," he wrote, "not much different from that of the Ethiopians." Note he didn't call them Indians (as did Columbus) or savages (as did so many Europeans).

Possibly, he was somewhere along the Carolina coast, or perhaps as far south as Georgia or even Florida.

> *Their hair is black and thick, and not very long. It is worn tied back upon the head, in the form of a little tail. In person they are of good proportions, of middle stature, a little above our own; broad across the breast, strong in the arms, and well formed in the legs and other parts of the body.*

We are left with a question: who were these people who resembled Ethiopians and were broad-chested, as we would expect of people in the Andes Mountains of South America?

> *They have broad faces but not all, however, as we saw many that had sharp ones, with large black eyes and a fixed expression. They are...acute in mind, active and swift of foot, as far as we could judge by observation. In these last two particulars they resemble the people of the East, especially those [that are] the most remote. We could not learn a great many particulars of their usages on account of our short stay....*

He did not speculate. He did not go beyond what he actually knew. I remember a lecture at a meeting of scholars about recognizing the limitations of one's knowledge. "The surest sign of scholarship," the speaker said, "is the ability to say 'I do not know.'"

Verrazano turned his ship around and sailed northward. Finally entering what is now called the Hudson River, his ship was anchored in the "Narrows." Verrazano and some of his shipmates took the ship's boat and rowed toward what is now lower Manhattan.

> *We came to a very pleasant situation among some steep hills, through which a very large river, deep at its mouth, forced its way into the sea.... Entering the river, we found the country on its banks well peopled, its inhabitants not differing much from the others, being dressed out with the feathers of birds of various colours. They came towards us with evident delight, raising loud shouts of admiration, and showing us where we could most securely land with our boat. We passed up this river, about half a league, when we found it formed a most beautiful lake three leagues in circuit, upon which they were rowing thirty or more of their small boats, from one shore to the other, filled with multitudes who came to see us.*

When a sudden wind arose, Verrazano and his men hastily rowed back to their ship, "greatly regretting to leave this region which seemed so commodious and delightful." They sailed away along the southern coast of present-day Long Island, and reached what is now known as Martha's Vineyard. He described it to King Francis as:

> *An island of triangular form … having many hills covered with trees, and well peopled, judging from the great number of fires which we saw all around its shores; we gave it the name of your Majesty's mother.*

Bad weather prevented their landing. They continued and found another island, with a "very excellent harbour." This was probably present-day Nantucket.

> *Before entering [the harbor], we saw about twenty small boats full of people, who came about our ship, uttering many cries of astonishment, but they would not approach nearer than within fifty paces; stopping, they looked at the structure of our ship, our persons and dress. Afterwards they all raised a loud shout together, signifying that they were pleased.… This is the finest looking tribe, and the handsomest in their costumes, that we have found in our voyage. They exceed us in size, and they are of a very fair complexion.… Their faces are sharp, their hair long and black, upon the adorning of which they bestow great pains; their eyes are black and sharp, their expression mild and pleasant.…*

Verrazano carefully related what he saw. With self-discipline he tried to avoid making suppositions about what he really did not know. Nor did he claim any land for a distant monarchy. He came, he saw, and he respected. That is a sign of wisdom. And this, also, is the traditional Lenape way. Observation without exaggeration, plus respect not only for what we see, but also for what we do not understand. We come into this world. We see it. And we need to respect it.

CHAPTER 7

NATIVES DISCOVER HENRY HUDSON

Eighty-five years—or three generations—after John Verrazano's voyage, Henry Hudson and his crew sailed from Amsterdam.

The French were already trading with natives. The English were a bit slow. The Dutch, more aggressive, sponsored an Englishman named Henry Hudson to explore a possible trade route to Asia. And so he mistakenly journeyed up the river that now bears his name. Their ship was called the *Half Moon*. Part of the crew was English, part Dutch. Robert Juet, a ship's mate, wrote about the voyage and George M. Asher translated Juet's document in 1860. We begin somewhere south of the Hudson River:

> *The seventeenth* (of August, 1609) *was all misty, so that we could not get into the harbour. At ten of the clock two boats came off to us, with six of the savages of the country, seeming glad at our coming. We gave them trifles, and they ate and drank with us; and told us that there were gold, silver, and copper mines hard*

> *by us; and that the Frenchmen do trade with them; which is very likely, for one of them spoke some words of French....*
>
> *The nineteenth ... The people coming aboard showed us great friendship, but we could not trust them.*
>
> *The twentieth ... we espied two French shallops* (boats designed for use on shallow water) *full of the country people come into the harbour, but they offered us no wrong, seeing we stood upon our guard. They brought many beaver skins and other fine furs, which they would have changed for red gowns... We kept good watch for fear of being betrayed by the people....*

Then, for no reason provided by Robert Juet, the Europeans ruthlessly vandalized and destroyed a small village:

> *The five and twentieth ... We manned our [boats] with twelve men and muskets ... and drove the savages from their houses, and took the spoil of them, as they would have done of us....*

Continuing onward, they repeatedly came into contact with friendly natives who had not heard of their criminal behavior down-river.

> *The people of the country came aboard ... seeming very glad of our coming, and brought green tobacco, and gave us of it for knives and beads. They go in deerskins loose, well dressed. They have yellow copper. They desire clothes, and are very civil.*
>
> *The fifth* (of September) *... Our men went on land ... and saw great store of men, women, and children, who gave them tobacco at their coming on land. So they went up into the woods, and saw great store of very goodly oaks and some currants. One of them came aboard and brought some dried [currants], and gave me some, which were sweet and good. This day many of the people came aboard, some in mantles of feathers, and some in skins of diverse sorts of good furs. Some women also came to us with hemp. They had red copper tobacco pipes, and other things of copper they did wear about their necks. At night they went on land again, so*

we rode very quiet, but [dared] not trust them..."

The next day began on a friendly basis. Then things went sour. Robert Juet is silent as to the cause. Hudson had sent a boat with five men to test the depth of a river some distance away. As they were returning, two large canoes with twenty-six natives closed in upon them. Alarmed, the Europeans may have struck first. One of Hudson's sailors, John Colman (who had previously scouted the land), died with an arrow in his throat. When the survivors finally reached their ship the anchor was lifted and they sailed away up the Hudson River.

Five days later, on the eleventh of September, they found another place to anchor their ship. "The people of the country came aboard of us," wrote Juet, "making show of love, and gave us tobacco and Indian wheat, and departed for that night." The next day twenty-eight canoes came toward the ship "full of men, women and children to betray us: but we saw their intent, and suffered none of them to come aboard...."

The Europeans sailed away. On September 15, as night was approaching, they tried another landing. Juet wrote: "We found very loving people, and very old men, where we were well used."

Sailing onward, three days later they anchored their ship once again. Juet wrote: "In the afternoon our master's mate went on land with an old savage, a governor of the country, who carried him into his house and made him good cheer...."

Henry Hudson and his first mate invited some of the "chief men" to board the boat. Their purpose, wrote Juet, was "to see if they had any treachery in them." He added that Henry Hudson and a ship's mate

> *...took them down into the cabin, and gave them so much wine and aqua vitae* (a strong alcoholic drink) *that they were all merry.... One of them had his wife with them, which sat so modestly as any of our country women would do in a strange place. In the end one of [the natives] was drunk ... and that was strange to them for they could not tell how to take it."*

After the party, the Europeans sailed northward and the river became shallow. The *Half Moon* then began the long journey back down the river and returned to Holland.

The English and Dutch sailors had found friendliness, hospitality, and trust. But some of the natives in one village discovered an ominous foreshadowing of things to come. Henry Hudson and his crew took what they had no ethical right to take. And although they hosted a jovial party where one of the unsuspecting natives was treated to enough alcoholic beverages to make him drunk, they merely laughed and made the natives think their intentions were good.

As for the Natives, they would eventually learn a bitter lesson. Hudson and his men destroyed only one village. The time would come, however, when white "friends" would destroy their culture, their ideals, and their future. There are some people who can make you feel very welcome and happy, but think carefully. Try to see if they genuinely care for your well-being and your future. Learn to perceive who is genuine and who is not. It can be difficult but it's crucially important. If their friendliness is not genuinely in your best interest, find a way of breaking away. Your future may depend upon your choices now.

CHAPTER 8

LIVING ON THE BACK OF A GIANT TURTLE

I've seen Native American pictures of life on the back of a giant turtle. A tree grows on a turtle's back. Clearly this is a symbol, a way of describing something profound in simple terms.

Human beings have an amazing ability to discern insight far beyond a simple picture. It's impossible to tell when people acquired this ability. Even Neanderthals had it. They buried at least some of their dead in a way that expressed love and respect for the deceased. They were able to look beyond what they saw with their eyes to what they felt in their heart. A corpse was more than just a dead body. There were cherished memories.

So when we hear "we live on the back of a giant turtle" we are hearing an idea that goes far beyond the picture of a turtle carrying a tree on its back. The tree is a symbol of endless forests where life is full of variety. No need to draw a detailed picture. Variety is part of the forests themselves. Look. Observe. Respect what you see. Some trees may have been growing before your grandfather was born. The rocks and stones may have been there since the planet was young. The life you see is established for sacrifice so other life may be born and grow.

Think.

But what of the turtle? Living on the back of a turtle is a way of describing the spiritual foundation upon which life thrives. The people—Lenape and other native nations—would thrive if they built their life upon a good, solid foundation. If Neanderthals possessed the ability to visualize ideas beyond the deceased body of someone they had cherished, certainly Lenape ancestors for thousands of years had the same ability. It's pitiful to lose this heritage by failing to explore beyond what we see and touch. Let's try to restore some of the spirit of long-ago people. Let's make it relevant for life in the twenty-first century!

Look again. Observe carefully.

Turtles live close to the earth. Their head can be raised toward the sky, but not too far. Sometimes we say someone is "down to earth." We mean this person has the capacity for common sense. People who are "down to earth" don't keep their heads in the clouds. They are not removed from reality. Without depriving themselves of high ideals, they plod ahead, one step at a time toward a goal that goes beyond where they are now. Worthwhile goals are not easily reached by a single leap.

One of Chief Bob Red Hawk's favorite expressions is "Walk softly and gently upon the earth, for she is your mother." More than something beautiful is gone when a landscape is torn apart. A landscape covered with grass and plants and trees is literally breathing in the carbon dioxide we breathe out, and replacing poisonous air with the oxygen we need for survival. Turtles live close to the earth. They walk softly and gently upon it. So should we.

Another idea derived from a turtle can be learned by taking a springtime walk along a forested creek to find a turtle basking in warm sunlight on a log in the water. Consider this. Some visitors who came into Lenape-hocking thought Indians were lazy. Men went hunting and fishing. Women took care of their gardens. Grandfathers shared wisdom from life experiences. Grandmothers watched and taught the children. Playing for fun was a human being's prerogative. They had time to think.

William Penn, founder of the colony of Pennsylvania, wrote, "They neither have much nor want much." Like a turtle, they took time for rest, comfort, leisure, and thinking. So should we.

Turtles are patient. They don't jump around like flies from one piece of excrement to another. By being patient, turtles avoid the mistake of hasty judgments and wrong conclusions. Our own life in the twenty-first century is bombarded with half-truths, no-truths, and some-truths. Too often, people believe a rumor without thinking or learning what is true, false, or somewhere in between. Some have their ears open more for something bad than something good. The best of the Lenape ancestors, like the turtle, took time to evaluate. So should we.

Once turtles decide to do something they move forward. They don't sit forever in the same place. And they never go backward.

Turtles are also humble, quiet creatures. The Lenape, like turtles, were not accustomed to raising their voices. Nor did they think they knew everything. Arrogance is unbecoming in any people who try to promote themselves at the expense of others. Arrogance of any kind is not the Lenape way.

Turtles are always, always, at home because they carry their home wherever they go. They have learned to live with themselves, not by deceptive self-confidence, but by accepting life with all its dangers and disappointments, and knowing what *can* be changed and what *can't*.

Are we comparing the intelligence of a turtle to that of a human being? Not really. We're using the turtle as a symbol of what life can be for ourselves.

Lenape ancestors felt in their hearts that living on the foundation of a symbolic turtle provides some of the most important ideals people can ever find. If we learn to live on the back of a giant turtle, we can do well. We can be high achievers in the highest achievement of all: living well with ourselves, with other people, and with the earth, sea, and sky. All this is included in living well with the Creator.

CHAPTER 9

FOREST PEOPLE

When the Pilgrims visited Cape Cod on November 11, 1620, they stopped briefly at an island. There were no Indians, yet William Bradford, the Pilgrim's governor at Plymouth, wrote they "found divers cornfields...." Indians had abandoned the place and gone to the mainland.

The Pilgrims also chose to leave Cape Cod and made their settlement at Plymouth. December, January, and February passed and Bradford wrote: "All this while the Indians came skulking about them, and would sometimes show themselves aloof. But when any approached near them, they would run away."

On March 16, 1621, an Indian named Samoset finally approached and became acquainted with the Pilgrims. "About four or five days after," wrote Bradford, he "came with the chief of his friends and other attendants." Weeks went by before women and children emerged. This seemed to be typical of northeastern Indian behavior when strangers entered their territory.

Let's look further.

Thirty-six years before, in 1584, Captains Arthur Barlowe and Philip Amadas took two ships and sailed from England. They anchored at an island off the coast of what is now Virginia. Barlowe wrote: "We remained by the side of this island two whole days before we saw any people of the country; the third day we espied one small boat rowing towards us, hauling in it three persons."

The boat stopped a distance away, and two of the men remained with it while the third approached the ships. He waited on land for Barlowe, Amadas, and some crewmen to approach him. They assured him of their friendship and he went on board one of the ships. Barlowe continued: "We ... gave him a shirt, a hat, and some other things, and made him taste of our wine, and our meat, which he liked very well." The Indian went and rejoined the two men he had left behind.

> *The next day there came unto us divers boats, and in one of them the king's brother, accompanied with forty or fifty men, very handsome and goodly people, and in their behavior as mannerly and civil as any in Europe.... A day or two after this we fell to trading with them.... After two or three days the king's brother came aboard the ships and drank wine, and eat of our meat and of our bread, and liked exceedingly thereof: and after a few days overpassed he brought his wife with him to the ships, his daughter and two or three children...."*

All of these meetings were part of a pattern. Woodland people retreated into the woods and silently observed visitors. Only after feeling assured they could meet on peaceful terms did they gradually reveal themselves.

The Dutch began settling upon the island of Manhattan during the

1620s. In 1628, Nicolas Jean de Wassenaer wrote about those first white settlers: "The population consists of two hundred and seventy souls.... They remained as yet without the fort, in no fear, as the natives live peaceably with them." During the time of William Penn this was also the way the Lenape lived with newcomers in Pennsylvania. They were hospitable and willing to share their land with strangers.

In 1684, three settlers in east Jersey (David Barclay, Arthur Forbes, and Gavin Laurie) combined their efforts to attract more settlers. As more settlers arrived, the Indians went further into the forests. The three settlers wrote: "There are but few Indian natives in this country.... They live in the woods, and have small towns in some places far up in the country." Before tensions became disruptive, the Indians moved quietly into the woods. In Pennsylvania, the Lenape followed this same peaceful tradition.

The forest was a place of protection. Natives had been hunter-gatherers for thousands of years, and knew how to return to those traditions. They also knew where to locate places of safety for their children and their women. Men who lived in or near the forest knew the backwoods because of their hunting experiences. Strangers were silently observed, their behavior scrutinized and evaluated. If newcomers seemed to be friendly, they received friendly hospitality. If the newcomers appeared to be belligerent, the Indians could paint their faces, shout the war-whoop to terrorize their enemies, and attack suddenly with overpowering strength. It is likely this method of warfare saved more lives than were lost, as brutality on a few would often scare the others away without wholesale slaughter.

White people hated this tactic because it was effective. An Indian raid was terrible, but was it not better than the European method of massive armies slaughtering large numbers of human beings in a single day while sometimes destroying an entire village along with all inhabitants?

The Lenape seldom went to war, and then only when pressures became unbearable. They traditionally practiced diplomacy. Along with neighboring Indian nations, their rhetorical skills were unsurpassed. They spoke honestly, from their heart, and could be trusted to keep their promises. Trade between many Indian nations was carried on at great distances. Messengers walked cross-country and regardless of their nationality went unharmed. But the Lenape—the People of the people—came to be esteemed above all others. They were called "grandfathers" because of their diplomatic skills and wise advice. Like all woodland nations, they were the Forest People.

There is much we can learn from the Lenape. Spirituality includes the wisdom to really observe those we are getting acquainted with. Diplomacy should take priority over confrontation. The quality of one's spirituality enables a person to speak courteously and from the heart. It also motivates a person to be someone who can be trusted to keep promises

CHAPTER 10

WILD-TURKEY PEOPLE

Traditional Lenape Indians believe a long and careful observation of an object in nature can be reflected in the character and personality of the observer. Is it really possible to become so intimate with something that we become like it ourselves?

The nineteenth century American writer, Nathaniel Hawthorne, apparently thought so. His story, "The Great Stone Face," is still popular in parts of New England and tells of a prophecy so old even the Indians handed the story down through the generations. The prophecy stated that one day a child would be born to become very noble and great, and would grow to resemble the Old Man on the

Mountain rock formation in Franconia Notch, New Hampshire.

In Hawthorne's story, a child named Ernest was told about the prophecy by his mother. Year after year, hour after hour, Ernest gazed in wonder at the very human-looking rock formation and waited for the prophecy to be fulfilled. Then, as he grew old and his hair turned white, a poet made the observation that Ernest himself had grown to be the very likeness of the Great Stone Face.

A Lenape clan mother told me her grandmother cherished a flower that was not very impressive on the outside but was beautiful deep within. Her grandmother was very much like that flower. I know a Lenape man who was fascinated by a melon and spent an entire growing season watching it grow. Like the melon, he is not only tender-hearted and good but solid enough for the stones of adversity to bounce harmlessly away.

The Unalachtigo people, a division of the Lenape, were known as the "Turkey clan" or, more appropriately, the "turkey phratry" (which means a group of clans). They lived in southern New Jersey and southeastern Pennsylvania. They were, like all Indians, careful observers of nature. Did they take to their hearts the wild turkey? It would not be surprising if they did. Although Unalachtigos no longer exist by that name, we can learn about the character of those ancient people by examining the animal that seems to have held so much of their attention.

The domesticated turkey is an object of derision. It's known chiefly as the main entrée at Thanksgiving dinners. It cannot fly because it is deliberately fattened for the table by overfeeding. It has no opportunity to use its brain, so the intelligence of its wild ancestors is gone.

Wild turkeys are entirely different. One day I was chatting with the director of a local historical society and the conversation veered toward wild turkeys because I was wondering why a group of Indians was named for them. She mentioned their ability to easily disappear into a forest. She told me, "I would see a small group of turkeys entering the woods. They would walk behind a tree and all of a sudden they were gone." That struck a chord with me. The Unalachtigo, as well as all woodland Indians, were especially adept at disappearing into the woods.

On the Internet, the Ohio State University Extension mentions that wild turkeys are courageous enough to challenge even an eagle in combat. The eagle is a predator and tries to seize young turkey chicks. We can be sure the Unalachtigo people had the same level of courage.

A poultry scientist in the Animal Sciences Department of Ohio State University once mentioned in an article the wild turkey's devoted awareness of its surroundings. The Unalachtigo, the wild-turkey people, would have had the same awareness.

Some stories describe turkeys as being so ignorant they actually drown staring at clouds while it's raining. Perhaps there is another interpretation. They hold their heads high to look at the sky, not entirely unlike the Unalachtigo people who held their heads high when they prayed. It was not from a lack of humility. All traditional Lenape believe they are invited to look up to heaven, toward the Creator, when they pray. Humbly and thankfully they trust that they are children of the Great Spirit.

Male turkeys walk proudly and spread their plumage. To this day, when Lenape wear beautiful regalia to pow wows, they are declaring that they are a beautiful people. Their regalia are evidence of their creativity because each is unique. They are rightfully unashamed of a spiritual heritage that may have begun twelve thousand or more years ago. It's not arrogance; it is a colorful expression of confidence in the Great Spirit's wish to make them people with strong and beautiful character.

Turkeys are social birds. They live and travel in groups. They spend most of their time earthbound but can run as fast as twenty miles an hour. They can fly close to earth as fast as fifty miles an hour, but only by first hopping along energetically, making the necessary effort to get off the ground. That provides an interesting observation on how to achieve success at anything, whether it's hunting and fishing, or whatever a person's goals are. Making good things happen takes time and energy.

Hawthorne's Ernest focused on a strong face that was full of character. From the symbol used to characterize them, we learn the

Unalachtigo courageously protected their young. They had vision that looked as high as the sky while, at the same time, they remained close to the reality of the earth. They would have been willing to reach toward a goal even if it required a great deal of effort. All this offers something worthwhile to think about as we continue to live our own lives.

CHAPTER 11

THE PEOPLE WHO KNEW WOLVES

David Brainerd was a Presbyterian missionary to the Lenape. He built his log cabin on a hill at what is now the town of Martins Creek, a few miles north of Easton, Pennsylvania. Brainerd's ministry in the 1740s was short (he died from tuberculosis at age 29) but far-reaching. He traveled by horseback to the Susquehanna River and met with people who knew wolves and were living on an island not far from present-day Sunbury, Pennsylvania. With little understanding of Lenape traditions—and no desire to learn them—he recorded the day's events of Sunday, September 21, 1745, in his journal:

> *Spent the day with the Indians on the island. As soon as they were well up in the morning I attempted to instruct them, and labored for that purpose to get them together; but soon found they had something else to do, for near noon they gathered together….. They were engaged for several hours, making all the wild,*

ridiculous and distracted motions imaginable; sometimes singing, sometimes howling.... I sat at a small distance, not more than thirty feet from them, though undiscovered, with my Bible in my hand, resolving, if possible, to spoil their sport....

What is especially interesting is David Brainerd's comment that they were "howling." I remember as a young boy being with other boys and howling like wolves. Nobody bothered to keep in tune, because there was no tune. We had a wonderful time! It was a lot of fun. Now, as I reminisce about it, I wonder if it was a little window that, just for a moment, opened into a long-ago world very different from our own.

North of the "Blue Mountains" which are between present-day Northampton and Monroe Counties in eastern Pennsylvania, there lived a separate nation of the Lenape known as the Munseys (also spelled Minsis, Munsees, Muncies, Minisinks). Munsee Lenape were the Wolf People. As the Turkey and Turtle People found much to observe and learn from turkeys and turtles, the Wolf People found much to observe and learn from wolves.

Research in recent decades has shown wolves to be caring, gentle, playful, courageous, intelligent, and social. I can't think of a better description of the Munseys. Old documents from various sources also reveal this likeness. Like the turkey and the turtle these characteristics are honored among all Lenape people.

Wolf pups learn from play the leadership qualities that will benefit them when they become adults. Wolves live in a close family unit. The father of a new-born pup, and sometimes others, brings food to the mother nursing the pup. All help in raising, teaching, or disciplining the young. Discipline is not severe but gentle and firm.

Wolves are curious and fascinated with objects. Not only the Munsey but all natives were eager to accept trinkets from European travelers.

Individual wolves are often called upon to sacrifice for the greater good of the pack. For example, an adult wolf may go hungry so that a pup may eat. Likewise, throughout Lenape-hocking, native chiefs saw to it that things were shared and no one went hungry.

Communication among wolves is sometimes unperceived by less-observant human beings. I can understand this. In my world, silence is often interpreted as agreement. Not necessarily in Lenape-hocking. Silence there may indicate it's time to pause and think more deeply.

And howling? Every wolf howls its own song, but howling together adds to the performance.

And so we can learn that play is an important ingredient in a person's well-being. So are sensitivity to the needs of others, gentleness instead of harshness, and courage in the face of adversity. Being socially-minded instead of being wrapped in one's own self-interest is an essential part of a healthy human spirit. Trinkets can be fun, but many Native Americans learned to their dismay dependence on that delight can also result in the loss of life's essentials. A balance between what is essential and nonessential should be maintained.

CHAPTER 12

WHO OWNS WHAT?

Questions about ownership have been a problem for untold thousands of years. The Lenape made progress in resolving that problem. "We own nothing" is a traditional Lenape saying. "Everything belongs to Creator." The sky above, the rivers and creeks, the land beneath our feet, the great variety of life, all come from Creator's vision. Every thing is a gift to be shared.

This belief is why Lenape ancestors were willing to share the land.

For a very long time the Lenape could not be convinced of what was happening before their eyes. Because the Lenape couldn't read the foreign language in deeds of land, even explanations of what they meant to Europeans did not sink in.

In contrast, Europeans thought they were purchasing *all* rights to the land, failing to appreciate the meaning of their own Bibles. Many Christians are familiar with Psalm 24:1 and yet fail to understand what it is really telling us: "The earth is the Lord's, and all that is in it, the world, and those who live in it" (New Revised Standard Version).

This European fixation on possession brought misunderstanding and tragic consequences that continue into the twenty-first century. The journal by writer, traveler, and Holland army master artilleryman David Pieterszoon de Vries, voyaging into the mouth of the Delaware River in 1632, is of special interest:

> *The second of December ... [we] smelled the land, which gave a sweet perfume as the wind came from the northwest..... This comes from the Indians setting fire, at this time of year, to the woods and thickets, in order to hunt; and the land is full of sweet-smelling herbs....*

The Lenape were sophisticated foresters. By carefully burning off the underbrush before it resulted in a great destructive conflagration, the forest was preserved and animal life would be abundant when the hunting season began the following autumn.

But de Vries and the other Dutchmen on board the ship were nervous. Hostilities were growing between the Lenape and the Dutch. Several Dutch settlers had already been killed and one of their houses, near present-day Lewes, Delaware, had been destroyed:

> *The eighth of December we sailed into the river before our destroyed house, well on our guard. The Indians came to the edge of the shore ... but dared not come in. At length, one ventured to come aboard ... whom we presented with a cloth dress, and told him we desired to make peace. Then immediately more came*

running aboard ... whom we presented with some trinkets.

They were told to return the next day with their chief so forgiveness and a firm peace could be established.

> *An Indian remained on board ... whom we asked why they had slain our people, and how it happened. He then showed us the place where our people had set up a column, to which was fastened a piece of tin, whereon the arms of Holland (depicting the Dutch lion defending Dutch territory) were painted. One of their chiefs took this off for the purpose of making tobacco-pipes, not knowing that he was doing amiss.*

The "column," with its tin shield bearing the Dutch coat of arms, declared the land was now under Dutch ownership and sovereignty.

> *Those in command at the house made such an ado about it, that the Indians, not knowing how it was, went away and slew the chief who had done it, and brought a token of the dead to the house to those in command, who told them that they wished they had not done it, that they should have brought him to them as they wished to have forbidden him to do the like again.*

It was a tragic misunderstanding. The Indian chief thought the tin shield was a gift to his people. The Dutch thought the land was now under the sovereignty of Holland. Some of the Natives, intent on establishing friendship with the visitors, had killed the unfortunate chief for upsetting their European guests. Native friends of the dead chief then took out their anger on the Dutch settlers who had created the uproar. If those visitors had known more of Native spirituality they might not have brought out their country's coat of arms in the first place.

No one owns anything. Everyone accepts with grateful hearts the gifts provided for them. As Creator gives bountiful gifts, so all creation is intended to share bountiful gifts. Those Lenape ancestors knew in their hearts we are all related. We are intended to cherish all these gifts in gratitude to the Creator who has created and shared them with us.

This is a very important part of Lenape spirituality.

CHAPTER 13

"IT'S SO FRUSTRATING!"

1643: a small colony of Swedes was struggling to exist in what is now the northeastern part of Delaware. Land purchases from the Minquas (a small group of Indians also known as the Susquehannocks) stretched the New Sweden colony for about fifty miles along the Delaware River near present-day Philadelphia. Both Minqua and Lenape Indians lived in adjacent small villages. A few English and Dutch settlers also lived in the area.

Johan Printz was sent as governor by the New Sweden Company to make the little colony profitable. In his book *The Swedes on the Delaware*, Amandus Johnson describes the instruction Governor Printz received before leaving Sweden:

> *Printz was instructed to keep peace with his neighbors as far as possible…... He was to try to supply the Indians with such articles as they needed and desired, and he was to endeavor to win their trade by underselling the English and Dutch. He was to treat [the Indians] with humanity and kindness, and to prevent his people from doing them any harm, so as to gain their confidence and goodwill. The beaver traffic was to be conducted for the benefit of the company….*

The Minquas spoke an Iroquois dialect. The Lenape used their own language. The English, Dutch, and Swedes, of course, clung to their own languages. It didn't take long for Governor Printz to become completely frustrated: "The Hollanders [Dutch] have fought the whole year with the savages," he wrote in his report to his corporate headquarters in 1644.

The Indians were expecting the type of trading relationship that required more colonists. "I have told them the whole year that we shall receive much people with our ships," wrote Governor Printz in his report.

The Indians considered a promise as a sacred covenant which should not be made lightly and *never* broken. When only one ship finally arrived—with no colonists and only a small supply of trading goods—Indian raiders took out their disappointment by killing two settlers and two soldiers. Whether these angry Indians were Minquas or Lenape, or both, we are not told. Governor Printz didn't care who they were. He was already utterly frustrated by the whole mess.

The inefficiency of the New Sweden Company increased his feeling of helplessness. The Swedish colonists were indifferent to his policies, English and Dutch settlers were a nuisance, and he could neither understand nor appreciate the completely different world of people still living in the Stone Age.

Trying to restrain his frustration was more than he could handle, and yet he could not ignore his orders from the New Sweden Company. Venting his anger, he wrote in his 1644 report:

> *Nothing would be better than that a couple of hundred soldiers should be sent here and kept here until we broke the necks of all of them in the river, especially since we have no beaver trade with them but only the maize (Indian corn) trade. They are a lot of poor rascals. Then ... when we have not only bought this river but also won it by the sword, no one — whether he be Hollander or Englishman — could pretend in any manner to this place either now or in coming times, but we should then have the beaver trade with the black and white Minquas alone, four times as good as we have had it.... If I should receive a couple of hundred good soldiers, then with the help of God not a single savage would be allowed to live in this river....*

Fortunately, neither God nor the New Sweden Company had the soldiers or the inclination to answer Printz's request. But at least he got his frustrations off his chest.

Two decades later, the colony of New Sweden was brought to an end by Dutch soldiers. The Minquas were conquered by the Iroquois. Eventually, most of the Lenape would retreat into western Pennsylvania and beyond.

Too many Indians tried to drown their sorrows and frustrations with rum and whiskey. But that only led to more demoralization.

I would like to raise these questions: What can we learn from this? Sooner or later, everyone experiences frustrations. How can they be handled? I really don't know, but there are a number of options: we can imitate Governor Printz and put our grievances into writing. We can rant and rave. We can bang our head against a wall. We can smash something. But for what purpose? Wouldn't it be better to think before we act rashly?

It's not helpful to bottle up frustrations, resentment, and anger. If we allow ourselves to feel victimized by circumstances or people, how can that lead us toward spiritual vitality? I wish there was an easy answer. Each person is unique and, as I see it, must persevere in finding his or her own unique way from frustration to inner peace. Perhaps by laying out all possible options from the simplest to the most complex, the easiest to the most difficult, a course of wisdom can be found.

Self-destruction in any form is not the answer. Neither is the destruction of someone else. It's our responsibility to find, instead, the way of self-*construction*—and not at the expense of someone else. Our spiritual goal includes recognizing our uniqueness and building on that, finding self-respect along the way.

CHAPTER 14

WISDOM WITHIN ROCKS

Mountains still guard the beautiful Delaware River as it flows between Pennsylvania and New Jersey. Mile after mile of magnificent grandeur catches the eye.

Not many miles north of Easton, Pennsylvania and Phillipsburg, New Jersey the river carves its way through the mountains at Delaware Water Gap. Geologists tell us that hundreds of millions of years before humans existed, the continent of North America collided into the continent of Africa, causing mountains to form and beginning the long process of creating the cleft that is the Gap. It makes one wonder: how long did it take before the Atlantic Creek became the Atlantic River and finally the Atlantic Ocean?

Rocks on these mountains have endured ice ages. Those in the valleys may have undergone the heavy steps of dinosaurs and mammoths. Bird-shrieks of long-extinct creatures have echoed among them. Many rocks were torn from their place of origin far in the north by huge glaciers covering hundreds of miles. Riding the backs of those glaciers, they were tumbled and crushed until the glacier melted and deposited them back to the earth.

Consider carefully the rocks! Modern physicists say rocks are bundles of energy, their atoms forming their own sub-microscopic universes.

Long after trees and four-legged animals arrived, two-legged people came to live among the rivers and forested mountains. For thousands of years their descendants cherished this world and pondered what they might learn if they watched and listened carefully. To sit and contemplate the rocks at one's feet, a person requires time and inclination. The Ancient Ones had both. They could not walk forever, they had to rest. And at sunset, as the daylight faded, they found the time to touch the rocks...*and think*.

The Ancient Ones could have no idea of the actual age of rocks, but they knew they were very old. They believed that, if able to speak, rocks could tell them something of Creator's purpose, since rocks were the very first to experience Creator's spirit.

For thousands of years people came and went, they intermarried, and they pondered the meanings of the silent rocks. If they had known what we know, would their feelings of awesome wonder have been even more intense?

Those who lived long ago sensed something beyond the hard surface of the rocks. They felt a living Presence, an ancient wisdom with no voice yet which spoke to their hearts. They had the same feelings as the poet of ancient Israel who wrote in Psalm 19 about the stars: "There is no speech, nor are there words; their voice is not heard; yet their voice goes out through all the earth" (New Revised Standard Version). A sense of awesome wonder is essential for both human spirituality and wisdom. The Ancient Ones knew this.

Consider the patient endurance of rocks. Think of existing in a hard and difficult environment, through all kinds of weather, yet unmoved by fear or worry! Patient endurance is a spiritual virtue and essential for wisdom.

Given human characteristics, the silent rocks witnessed events, heard the prayers of passersby, and were sometimes piled to form a monument. Yet they never tell their secrets. Is this a lesson that combines wisdom *and* spirituality? Think about it.

Furthermore, rocks have endured the slow erosion of passing years. Nothing remains the same forever, yet rocks serenely tolerate the passage of time. This, also, is a lesson in spirituality that bravely faces the future as time passes inexorably along.

Rocks may be scattered far and wide, and may be similar yet different. Even those from far-off places co-mingle with those that have always been there. There is wisdom as well as spirituality to be found in this! A solitary rock does not make a majestic mountain. Nothing lives by itself alone. Likewise, no civilization can remain healthy when individuals seek only their own self-interest.

The Lenape were individualists. Many of their villages were separated by mountains covered with dense forests, yet the people moved back and forth. Family relatives were widespread, countless trails found their way through the mountainous wilderness, and messengers of every tribe were given safe passage. This is evidence for communication despite nature's obstacles.

There is a balance that needs to be maintained between individualism and togetherness, and the ancestors of long ago, profound observers of their environment, realized that equilibrium. They balanced their individuality with concern for the common good. Wisdom and spirituality function together.

Throughout the history of all people there have been failures as well as successes. European civilization experienced the Dark Ages that were followed by a renaissance. Lenape tradition tells of long painful periods when spirituality and wisdom were neglected. But in the times of their greatness, they thoughtfully observed and learned from the earth around them.

The wisdom found in rocks, perceived by the Lenape, points to some of the spiritual requirements necessary for building a civil civilization. We, too, can observe and learn patient endurance, the honoring of secrets, serenity in the midst of the slow erosion of passing years, to live without distorting our world with self-centered self-interest, and to uphold our own individuality balanced with holding friendships together.

Spirituality and wisdom are inseparable. With awesome wonder, they see beyond what is seen with the eye and touched with the hand.

CHAPTER 15

A CHAIN OF FRIENDSHIP

The Swedish colony of New Sweden came under Dutch rule in 1655 and became part of the New Netherland Colony, which ended in 1667 when taken over by the British. In 1674, the British also took control of the small settlement of New Amsterdam and renamed it New York in honor of James, the Duke of York.

William Penn was a member of the often-persecuted Christian group called The Friendly Association (also known as Quakers). King Charles II owed 16,000 pounds to William's father, a debt which passed to William when his father died. William had long hoped to go to America and establish a place where people would be free to think their own thoughts about religion and spirituality. He followed the right channels, knew the right people, and agreed to the cancellation of the royal debt in return for the right to establish a colony in what would become Pennsylvania.

But there was a problem. People were already living there: the

Swedish, the Dutch, the English, other Europeans, and natives who had been there thousands of years before anyone else. William Penn strove to solve the problem by establishing a government where everyone would live peacefully together.

In October, 1681, while still living in London, he wrote a letter that was sent by ship to all leaders of the native population who could be gathered together. Nothing can better express William Penn's hope than his own words. Because he wanted it translated and interpreted in the best way possible, and in the interest of clarity for this book, archaic spellings, punctuation, and paragraphing have been modified to twenty-first century form:

> *My friends: There is one great God and Power that has made the world and all things therein, to whom you and I and all people owe their being and well-being, and to whom you and I must one day give an account for all that we do in this world.*
>
> *This great God has written his law in our hearts, by which we are taught and commanded to love and help and do good to one another, and not to do harm and mischief to one another.*
>
> *Now this great God has pleased to make me concerned in your parts of the world. The king of the country where I live has given to me a great province [in your part of the world], but I desire to enjoy it with your love and consent, that we may always live together as neighbors and friends. Else what would the great God say to us, who has made us not to devour and destroy one another but live soberly and kindly together in the world?*
>
> *…I am very sensible of the unkindness and injustice that has been too much done toward you by the people of these parts of the world. They have sought to take great advantages of you, rather than be examples of justice and goodness to you. I heard [this] has been a matter of trouble to you, and caused great grudges and animosities, sometimes to the shedding of blood. [This] has made God angry.*
>
> *But I am not such a man, as is well known in my own country. I have great love and regard toward you, and I desire to*

win and gain your love and friendship by a kind, just, and peaceable life. And the people I send are of the same mind, and shall in all things behave themselves accordingly. And if anything shall offend you or your people, you shall have a full and speedy satisfaction ... by an equal number of honest men on both sides, that by no means you may have occasion of being offended against them.

I shall shortly come to you myself. At that time we may ... freely confer and discuss these matters. In the meantime I have sent my commissioners to negotiate with you about land and a firm guarantee of peace. Let me desire you to be kind to them and the people, and receive the presents and tokens which I have sent to you as a testimony of my goodwill to you, and my resolution to live justly, peaceably, and friendly with you.
I am your friend,
William Penn

His letter was well received by the Lenape. What was close to the heart of William Penn was also close to their heart. Yes, every civilization has people who are uncivil. Every Christian congregation has members who neglect the teachings of Jesus. Every religion includes people who do not adhere to its best teachings. This has always been and always will be. By the same token, there will always be those to who willingly reveal the best of their religious and spiritual traditions.

For generations afterward, even in the worst of times, there were Lenape who fondly remembered the hopes of William Penn and their own ancestors. They called it the Chain of Friendship. It is mentioned in treaty negotiations time and time again. Sometimes in the picturesque language of the Lenape, the chain became rusty. Sometimes it broke and had to be repaired. But for over a hundred years, documents of that era reveal their desire to repair, polish, and renew the Chain of Friendship.

William Penn's optimism for people of different traditions, different languages, and different opinions living amicably together, illustrates that no civilization worthy of the name can allow goodwill to die. There are chains of friendship that need to be repaired, polished and kept from becoming rusty wherever we live.

Think of it. Consider what you can do and say to make this happen.

CHAPTER 16

VISION FOR NOW AND ALWAYS

Before William Penn came to Pennsylvania he was interested in the southwestern part of what is now New Jersey. After taking this land from the Dutch, who had taken it from the Swedes, King Charles II of England gave it to Penn. It was there William Penn's vision of religious freedom first took root. In *The Concessions and Agreements of the Proprietors, Freeholders, and Inhabitants of the Province of West New Jersey in America*, a constitution signed by Penn and others in 1676, article 12 states:

> *There is likewise certain provision made for the liberty of conscience in matters of religion, that all persons living peaceably*

may enjoy the benefit of the religious exercise thereof without any molestation whatsoever.

Freedom of religion eventually became part of the Bill of Rights in the Constitution of the United States of America.

In 1682, William Penn entered Pennsylvania. The next year he wrote to the Society of Traders in London and included a description of his thoughts about the Lenape:

> *We have agreed that in all Differences between us, Six of each side shall end the matter. Don't abuse them, but let them have Justice, and you win them.... [The Indians] kindly received me, as well as the English who were few before the people concerned with me came among them. I must needs commend their respect to authority and kind behaviour to the English.... As they are people proper and strong of body, so they have fine children, and almost every house full; rare to find one of them without three or four boys and as many girls.... And I must do them that right, I see few young men more sober and laborious.*

But already he recognized all was not well. Not every Swedish and Dutch settler had treated the Indians fairly. William Penn wrote with disgust to his acquaintances in London:

> *The worst is, that [the Lenape Indians] are the worse for the Christians, who have propagated their vices, and yielded them tradition for ill, and not for good things....*

He prayed Christians who claimed to have a better knowledge of the Deity than the Indians would surpass the Indians in spirituality:

> *I beseech God to incline the hearts of all that come into these parts to outlive the knowledge of the natives, by a fixed obedience to their greater knowledge of the will of God. For it were miserable indeed for us to fall under the just censure of the poor*

Indian conscience, while we make profession of things so far transcending.

It did not happen as he hoped. Nevertheless, this provides significant information about Lenape spirituality at this time in history. Europeans knew their technology was superior to that of the native population, and they wanted to believe the way they practiced their religion was superior also. But too many Europeans professed Christianity without embracing the *heart* of Christianity. And how is a religion with only creeds and dogma better than spirituality holding goodwill, fairness, and honesty close to one's heart?

William Penn confessed his doubts about some Swedish, Dutch, and English settlers. He had already become acquainted with native people who exemplified goodwill, fairness, and honesty. He knew how his fellow Europeans cheated in business and gave financial profit priority over commercial integrity. It would not be long before he would have to return to England to settle a financial mess created by one of his own business associates.

In his dealings with the Lenape he did not find problems of self-centered greed, but he did express a concern that they could all too quickly learn the way of Europeans.

By 1691, William Penn's holdings reached all the way into present-day Lancaster County. On July 16, 1691, he sold 375 acres of rich farmland not far from the Susquehanna River to Henry Maydock of Chester County. William Penn had acquired the land honestly. Indians were willing to share farmland because they were more interested in hunting the forested mountains and fishing the rivers and streams. Knowing this, William Penn hoped Europeans and Indians could accommodate themselves in a long-enduring friendship with no need to quarrel over who lived where.

But every visionary needs people who will follow toward the high purpose of that vision. When William Penn died, it seemed his hope for goodwill, fairness, and honesty died with him. His own sons would later betray all the good he had accomplished.

Nevertheless, William Penn's vision was not completely lost.

Freedom of conscience in religious matters eventually became part of the Constitution, and still thrives as a symbol of civil civilization. The goal of integrity in commerce can be found when worthwhile government regulations restrict the greed that distorts commerce.

The Lenape have a tradition of looking ahead to "the seventh generation." People in each generation are responsible not only for the quality of life now but for the next seven generations.

One self-centered generation can break the flow for future generations. We will find ample evidence of this in the generation that followed William Penn's. And yet the vision can continue. Each person is responsible for breaking the bonds of ill-will and self-centeredness so the vision can be refreshed and renewed.

In generation after generation, that long-range vision is imperative. Goodwill, fairness, and honesty make spirituality genuine. Every individual and every government is responsible for making contributions to the quality of life both now and for future generations. This vision, like William Penn's, can find its way into the future, into places as yet unimagined. This confident hope is part of traditional Lenape spirituality.

CHAPTER 17

TAMANEND – AND A CIVIL CIVILIZATION

The Merriam-Webster Dictionary defines *civilization* as, "A relatively high level of cultural and technological development; specifically: the stage of cultural development at which writing and the keeping of written records is attained." The definition further states, "Refinement of thought, manners, or taste."

We may need to be careful how we define *refinement*. If someone exhibits impeccable manners at a dinner party, but then in business is a cut-throat, ruthless executive capable of abusing employees, customers, competitors, or stockholders, I do not call that refinement. If someone is adept at black-tie social events but rude to people who are not in the same economic status, please don't call that refinement. If someone is an excellent but impatient and aggressive automobile driver, they are neither excellent nor refined.

The word *civilization* begins with *civil*, and isn't that what civilization is really all about?

When the Moravian missionary John Heckewelder described Tamanend, the Unami-Lenape chief who welcomed William Penn, he used memories going back more than one hundred thirty years. Heckewelder was a careful scholar, however, and not likely to exaggerate:

> *All we know, therefore, of Tamanend is, that he was an ancient Delaware (Lenape) chief, who never had his equal. He was in the highest degree endowed with wisdom, virtue, prudence, charity, affability, meekness, hospitality, in short with every good and noble qualification that a human being possesses.*

The Apostle Paul, in his letter to the Christians in Galatia over 1,700 years before, described such qualities as "living by the Spirit." Heckewelder may have had this in mind when he added that Tamanend had in his heart a close association with the "great and good Spirit; for he was a stranger to everything that is bad." Heckewelder continued:

> *The fame of this great man extended even among the whites.... In the Revolutionary war, his enthusiastic admirers dubbed him a saint, and he was established under the name of St. Tammany, the patron saint of America.*

The sometimes corrupt political organization of New York City's Tammany Hall (1789-1965) attempted to capitalize upon his fame but their efforts fell far short of Tamanend's true character.

Archaeological evidence points to the peacefulness of the Lenape character. Other tribes often used protective wooden poles around their villages, evidenced by wood particles left behind when they decayed. The obvious lack of protective poles around Lenape villages infers either the Lenape were powerful enough to discourage invasion, had created few enemies, or both. Documents of William Penn's era and the preceding colonies of New Sweden and New Netherland indicate violence for the Lenape was by far the exception to the rule.

When Tamanend and his Councilors were negotiating with William Penn over Penn's requests for purchasing land, their thinking was based upon their belief in Creator's ownership of land and sky. For all his good intentions, however, William Penn was limited to the European notion of land ownership: all rights and privileges became the sole property of the owner.

Instead of selling away all rights to the land, ancient Lenape thought they were sharing the land, and the presents given them were considered tokens of gratitude, for which they were very grateful. An old newspaper clipping entitled "In Memory of Tammany" I found in *The Book Shelf Scrap Book of Easton and Northampton County* at the local history room of the Easton, Pennsylvania Public Library, illustrates this point by mentioning Tamanend and his people sold the same land "three times to William Penn in 1683, 1692, and 1697."

Considering Tamanend was noted for honesty and integrity, we might wonder why William Penn paid three times for the same land. It helps to remember the Lenape concept of Creator's ownership. The few items they received for their land did not show ignorance of the land's value but was testimony to their commitment of sharing Creator's creation. They anticipated, and were grateful for, the presents they received from time to time as gifts of appreciation for their continuing hospitality.

The Book Shelf Scrap Book of Easton and Northampton County also contains an excerpt from a speech made by Tamanend at a council in Philadelphia on July 6, 1694, twelve years after his first contact with William Penn. The Iroquois to the north wanted the Lenape to attack white settlers because of some disagreements. Tamanend and his council rejected the invitation to war and emphasized the spiritual quality of forgiveness.

In the colorful language of the Lenape, Tamanend told the Council::

We and the Christians ... have always had a free roadway to one another, and, though sometimes a tree has fallen across the road, yet we have still removed it ... and kept the path clear, and we design to continue the old friendship that has been between us and you.

The hospitable, forgiving spirit of the Lenape was long and enduring. It took many years before the patience of some finally wore out, mostly due to the horrendous abuse of their traditional hospitality by the sons of William Penn.

Tamanend and William Penn showed a sophisticated, intelligent appreciation of the spirituality essential for a great civilization where civilized people are sensitive to their relationship to the world and everyone around them. Civilized people are therefore civil.

Isn't that just as true now as it was several hundred years ago?

CHAPTER 18

TAMANEND:
AMERICA'S PATRON SAINT

Long after William Penn first met him in 1682, Tamanend was still held in such high esteem among settlers they called him "the Patron Saint of America." Is it possible to be a saint without ever being known to be a Christian?

Many, including William Penn, referred to Lenape chiefs as "kings." This is very misleading. They were not monarchs. Lenape civilization was democratic. No decisions were made without careful thought and conference in the village council. Women were honored and highly respected. *They* decided who would be chief. If a fight broke out among the males, women could command them to stop, and they would obey.

Village chiefs were chosen to serve, not command. Lenape tradition believed all chiefs should be genuine servants of—and for—the people. When men returned from a successful hunting expedition they gave their successes to the chief who distributed the bounty to everyone according to their needs, the elderly receiving priority. Everyone was "paid" for their work with the knowledge they were helping—not hurting—Creator's creation. Success was not measured by the wealth of their pocketbooks, but by the genuine goodness of their hearts.

William Penn, however, could not get the idea of *monarchy* out of his mind. It was the only form of government he had ever known. In this strange land, he came face to face with an entirely different way of governing:

> *Every king has his council; and that consists of all the old and wise men of his nation.... Nothing of moment is undertaken, be it war, peace, selling of land, or traffic, without advising with them, and ... with the young men too.*

Because he wanted to purchase land instead of seizing it, William Penn met frequently with village councils. In writing about one such meeting, he described a scene where older and wiser council members sat in a semi-circle facing their chief, while the inexperienced young men sat respectfully behind them.

After William Penn made his request to purchase land, the Council members consulted among themselves. Finally, the chief ordered someone to speak on his behalf. The man appointed to speak...

> *...stood up, came to me, and in the name of the king saluted me, then took me by the hand, and told me that he was ordered by his king to speak to me, and that now it was not he but the king who spoke....*

The man then proceeded to discuss the boundaries of the land and the presents that were anticipated.

> *During the time this person spoke, not a man of them was observed to whisper or smile—the old grave, the young reverent in their deportment. They speak little, but fervently, and with elegance.*

A Lenape Council always maintained decorum and upheld respect. Deep-seated emotions were present, but the members knew how to control them. Only he who held the "talking stick" was allowed to speak. Everyone had an opportunity to express an opinion, but no one would interrupt the one speaking.

Contrary to what sometimes happens in political maneuvering, nothing was "railroaded" through. A consensus was more important than having winners and losers. Tamanend and his people had the patience to be courteous. "I have never seen more natural sagacity," William Penn said in a salute to their intelligence.

The turtle's slowness was preferred to the rabbit's swiftness. They were people still living in the Stone Age, yet their manners were superior to some in meetings held even now, more than three hundred years later—especially superior to today's political campaigns where candidates toot their own horns and distort their opponent's positions.

The Council meeting concluded with sincere vows of friendship. Again quoting from William Penn's description:

> *When the purchase was agreed, great promises passed between us of kindness and good neighbourhood, and that the Indians and English must live in love, as long as the sun gave light.*

Tamanend and his people remembered the quarrels between the Swedes and Dutch (or Hollanders as they were called). They also remembered how often they were cheated. William Penn promised he and his people would be different. And in Lenape culture a promise was a sacred covenant. Referring to himself, Penn wrote:

> *...having now such an one that had treated them well, they should never do him or his any wrong. At every sentence of which they shouted, and said Amen in their way.*

The house he built for himself, known as "Pennsbury Manor," still stands in its undefended location in Pennsylvania. It is a silent testimony to trust and friendship that needed no defense against enemies.

Tamanend is remembered as the "Patron Saint of America." From old documents like those quoted here, we can learn much about the qualities of leadership still needed by anyone who wishes to become a genuine leader and a genuine human being.

CHAPTER 19

IMAGINE!

Imagine we have a time machine that can whisk us back well over 300 years. Imagine we can interview some eyewitnesses to great historic moments! They can speak to us through the power of the written word.

In 1681, *William Penn* arrived in what would become Pennsylvania. He had been given land by King Charles II and his brother, the future King James II, as a way of paying debts owed to his father's estate. Penn, however, decided to earn the trust of the native people by negotiating land purchases with them. He also learned their language.

Francis Daniel Pastorius was born and educated in Germany. He was twenty-five years old when William Penn met him on a trip through Germany. Attracted by Penn's sincere spirituality, Pastorius left Europe for America a year after Penn. Francis Daniel Pastorius founded Germantown near Philadelphia and, like Penn, welcomed the Lenape into his home.

Gabriel Thomas was twenty years old when he joined William Penn's people on their journey to America. He wrote a book about Pennsylvania and returned to London to see it published. A few years later, he returned to America and lived in Philadelphia until his death in 1714.

Using our imaginations we'll ask these men who were well acquainted with Lenape Indians some questions and "listen" as they begin to speak again through excerpts of their own writings.

We will number our questions in the Unami dialect of the Lenape, as William Penn and his associates heard it and recorded it. We will listen to our guests' replies not in the manner of the 1690s, but in a more modernized style. We will avoid, for example, the word *savage* and substitute the original meaning of Lenape: "People of the Forest."

Question *Kooty* (One): *When you first saw them what did they look like?*

Penn: "They are generally tall, straight, well-built and mostly walk with a lofty chin. Of complexion, black, but by design. They grease themselves with bear's fat, and having no defense against sun or weather their skins are swarthy. Their eye is little and black and I have seen handsome European-like faces among them. When they travel in the woods, at night they sleep around a great fire, with the mantle of coarse cloth they wear by day wrapped around them. They put a few small tree branches around them to warn them of a wild animal's approach."

Pastorius: "They are generally tall of stature, with powerful bodies, strong shoulders, austere foreheads, and paint their faces red, blue, etc., in various ways. They have no beards. They have coal-black hair, shave their head, and allow a long lock to grow on the right side. They went naked at first with only a cloth about their loins. Now they are beginning to wear shirts. In winter they hang mantles of coarse cloth around themselves. They also smear the children with bear grease, and let them creep about in the heat of the sun so that they become the color of a nut, although they were at first white by nature. They are people of the forest who instruct and teach one another by means of tradition, from the aged to the young."

Thomas: "They will not allow their beards to grow, for they pluck the hair off with their own fingers as soon as they can get hold of it, believing it a great deformity to have a beard."

Question *Nisha* (Two): *When you came to live here, aliens in their land, how did they react to you?*

Pastorius: "The first who came before my eyes were two men who came in a canoe to our ship. I presented them with a dram of brandy. They attempted to pay me for it with a sixpence, and when I refused the money they gave me their hands, and said 'Thank you, brother.' I was once dining with William Penn when one of their chiefs sat at table with us. William Penn, who can speak their language very fluently, said to him that I was a German. He visited me on the third of October. On the twelfth of December another chief and his wife came. Also many other persons visit very often, to whom I often show my love with a piece of bread and a drink of beer, whereby an answering affection is awakened in them and they call me *carissimo*—meaning brother."

Penn: "If a European comes to see them, or calls for lodging at their *wigwam*, they give him the best place and first cut of meat. If they come to visit us, they salute us with an *Itah* which means "Good be to you," and sit themselves down, which is mostly on the ground close to their heels, their legs upright. Maybe they speak not a word more, but observe everything. If you give them anything to eat or drink, well, for they will not ask. And be it little or much, if it be with kindness, they are well pleased."

Thomas: "They do not like to be asked twice about the same thing.

They are very loving to one another. They are also very kind and civil to any Christian. For I myself have had meat cut by them in their *wigwams*, before they took any for themselves."

These voices from the distant past speak again and we learn about hospitality. We learn about bridging the gaps between social, cultural, religious, and other differences. Being willing to overcome gaps like these is a virtue that reveals an inward spirituality, a worthy example in any day or age.

CHAPTER 20

LINGERING A LITTLE LONGER

Let's not be in a hurry to leave our time machine that helps us hear eyewitnesses as the year 1700 is approaching. From their own writings we can extend our interview with William Penn, Francis Daniel Pastorius, and Gabriel Thomas. We continue with numbering questions in the language of the Lenape at that long-ago time.

Question *Nach* (Three): *You've heard them talk and all three of you have learned their language. Tell us about it and please try to leave your archaic words behind! Remember, four hundred years have passed since you've been here.*

Thomas: "As to the manner of their language, it is high and lofty, with a short sentence. Their way of counting is by tens, as to say 'two tens,' 'three tens,' 'four tens,' 'five tens,' etc. Their language is elegant, but not copious. Of noble sound and accent. Take here a specimen:

'Hodi hita nee huska a peechi, nee, machi,
Pennsylvania huska dogwachi, keshow a peechi
Nowa, huska hayly, Chetena koon peo.'

Thus in English:

'Farewell, friend, I will very quickly go to
Pennsylvania. Very cold moon will come presently,
And very great hard frosts will come quickly."

Pastorius: "Their language is very dignified. They are of few words, and are amazed when they perceive so much unnecessary chatter, as well as other foolish behavior on the part of the Christians."

Penn: "Their language is lofty, yet narrow like short-hand writing. One word serves in the place of three, and the rest are supplied by the understanding of the hearer. I have made it my business to understand it, that I might not need an interpreter on any occasion; and I must say that I know not a language spoken in Europe that has words of more sweetness or greatness, in accent and emphasis, than theirs."

Question *Neo* (Four): *What about their religious beliefs? Some of our folks say they're heathen and have no religion. Others say that if religion is a matter of creeds and dogma, they have none."*

Penn: "They believe in a God and in immortality—without the help of theologians. They say there is a great chief that made them, who dwells in a glorious country to the southward, and that the souls of the good shall go thither, where they shall live again."

Pastorius: "They know of no idols, but they worship a single all-powerful God who limits the power of the Devil. They say that God dwells in the most glorious southern land, to which they also shall go at some future time after death. After the course of life is finished they will have a suitable recompense from the all-powerful hand of God awaiting them. They have two kinds of worship, namely in song and sacrifices. They slaughter the first fruits of their hunting as a sacrifice with such vigor that the whole body sweats. When they sing, they dance around in a circle."

Penn: "Their singing is performed by round-dances, sometimes words, sometimes songs, then shouts, two being in the middle that begin, and by singing and drumming on a board they direct the chorus. This is done with equal earnestness and labor, but great appearance of joy."

Pastorius: "They accompany their worship of God with songs, during which they make strange gestures and motions with their hands and feet."

Thomas: "They observe New Moons. They offer their first fruits to a deity, whereof they have two: one, as they believe, is above and good, and another below who is bad."

Penn: "In the fall, when the corn is harvested, they begin to feast. There have been two great festivals already, to which all come who want to. I was at one myself. Their entertainment was a green seat by a spring, under some shady trees. They had twenty male deer, with hot cakes made of new corn, both wheat and beans, which they made up in a square form in the leaves of the stem, and bake them in ashes. And after that they began dancing. Those that go must carry a small present which is made from the bone of a fish, with the black color more precious than white, and they call it *wampum*."

Question *Pelenach* (Five): *And do they practice their religion, or spirituality, in their daily life?*

Penn: "In liberality they excel. Nothing is too good for their friend. Give them a fine gun, coat, or something else, and it may go through twenty hands before someone finally keeps it."

Pastorius: "One must distinguish them into those who had associated for some time with the so-called Christians and those who are just beginning to come forth out of their villages. For the former are crafty and deceitful, which they learned from the above-mentioned nominal Christians. Such a person said he would bring me a turkey, but in its place he brought an eagle and wished to persuade me that it was a turkey. When, however, I showed him that I had seen many eagles he acknowledged to a Swede who stood nearby that he had done it out of deception, in the belief that because I had arrived here only recently I would not know such birds so accurately. But those who have only recently come out of their villages are of a reasonable spirit, injure nobody, and we have nothing to fear from them.... When we Christians are not provided for a month, how unhappy we are, while these 'heathen' have such a wonderful spirit that they attribute their sustenance to God."

These congenial relationships are quite different than those that would exist sixty years later when the frontier was still in Pennsylvania. It will be helpful to explore further what relationships were like in the time of William Penn.

CHAPTER 21

MORE TIME WITH EYE-WITNESSES

Continuing with our time machine, we inquire more deeply into the character of Lenape life just before the year 1700 from the writings of William Penn, Francis Daniel Pastorius, and Gabriel Thomas. We'll also continue to use the Lenape language of that time as we number our questions.

Question *Koottash* (Six): *Are you sure those people could be trusted?*

Pastorius: "They live more contentedly and with less thought for the morrow than we Christians. They cheat no one in business. They also know nothing of the fashions in clothes to which we cling so closely. They neither curse nor swear, are temperate in their food and drink, and if one occasionally drinks too much it is usually the nominal Christians who are to be blamed, who for their own self-interest sell strong drink to the forest people."

Penn: "Don't abuse them, but let them have justice, and you win them."

Pastorius: "In my ten years of residence here I have never heard that they have attempted to do violence to anyone, far less murdered anyone, although they have not only had frequent opportunity to do so, but would also have been able to conceal themselves in the thick and extensive forest. We do not need to be afraid of any sudden attack on the part of these native inhabitants, as they are quite humane and respectful to all strangers coming to them."

Thomas: "They generally delight much in mirth."

Pastorius: "They strive after a sincere honesty, hold strictly to their promises, willingly give shelter to others, and are useful and loyal to their guests. But our nominal Christians are diametrically opposed to these 'heathen' virtues and seek their pleasure in eating, drinking, gambling, and debauchery; in usury, fraud, envy, cursing, and quarreling."

Thomas: "The Indians are very studious in observing the virtues of roots and herbs, by which they cure themselves of many sicknesses in their bodies, both internal and external."

Pastorius: "As for their livelihood, the men attend to their hunting and fishing. The women bring up their children honestly, under careful oversight, and admonish them against sin. They plant Indian corn and beans around their huts. They are astonished that we Christians take so much trouble and thought concerning eating and drinking and comfortable clothing and houses, as if we doubted that God would care for us."

Question *Nishash* (Seven): *What don't you like about them, and is there anything else you'd like to say?*

Pastorius: "They do not work willingly, but support themselves by hunting and fishing, and not one of them is accustomed to riding a horse."

Thomas: "They are reserved, and apt to resent and retain their resentment for a long time."

Pastorius: "In summer they do not cover themselves, except what nature wishes covered. In winter they wrap themselves up in a coarse square cloth. In their huts they cover themselves with bear and dear skins. Instead of shoes they use thin deer skin, and they have no hats."

Penn: "The worst is that they are the worse for Christians who have propagated vices instead of doing good things. Since these Europeans came the Indians have become lovers of strong liquors, rum especially. To get it they exchange the best of their animal skins and furs. If they are heated with liquors they are restless until they have enough to sleep. And when drunk they are one of the most wretched spectacles in the world."

Pastorius: "And yet it may be stated in reply that so far as I have gone among them, I have found them reasonable people and capable of understanding good teaching and manners, who can give evidence of an inward devotion to God."

Penn: "They care for little, because they want but little. We sweat and toil to live; their pleasure is in hunting and fishing."

Thomas: "They also make Indian mats, ropes, hats, and baskets of their hemp, which grows wild and natural in the woods in great plenty. Their women are very ingenious in their several employments, as well as the men."

Penn: "In sickness they are impatient to be cured; and give anything for a cure, especially for their children, to whom they are extremely attached. At times they drink a concoction of some roots in spring-water. And if they're sick and eat any meat it must be of the female of any creature."

Thomas: "If a friend dies they don't allow mentioning the friend's name. They also paint their face with black lead. But when things go well with them they paint their faces with red lead, it being a sign of their joy, as the other is a sign of their grief."

Penn: "They continue mourning for a year. They carefully choose the graves for their dead, lest they be lost by time; they pick off the moss that grows upon them and heap up the earth with great care and exactness."

Pastorius: "We Christians in Germantown and Philadelphia no longer have the opportunity to associate with them, in view of the fact that their chiefs of the forest have accepted money from William Penn and, together with their people, have withdrawn far away from us into the wild forest."

Thomas: "The Dutch and Swedes inform us that they are greatly decreased in number to what they were when they first came into this country. And the Indians themselves say that two of them die to every one Christian that comes in here."

Pastorius: "In conclusion, I must add that they are much against war and the shedding of human blood, and would far rather be at peace with all; while in contrast, nearly all of Christendom is under arms, and they rend and destroy one another in offensive and defensive warfare with barbaric cruelty!"

CHAPTER 22

PROMISES

The years went by. Many eye-witnesses from the time of William Penn—including Mr. Penn himself—crossed over (died). New people arrived. Probably no one ever imagined how many Europeans wanted to get away from the economic, religious, and political stresses of their home countries.

In Lenape-hocking, native people were becoming increasingly uneasy about the overwhelming influx of immigrants. There was no end to the shiploads of strangers disembarking at the Port of Philadelphia, pledging allegiance to an unseen ruler of a country far across the ocean, and taking the best farmland. While the Indians preferred forests, hills, and rivers for hunting and fishing, the calendar had hardly turned to the year 1700 before some Indians began moving westward.

Friendly settlers sometimes accompanied Indians on hunting expeditions, but Lenape men kept some secrets to themselves: They bathed every night, and ate no meat for three days before hunting to ensure they were free from body odor. Their white neighbors, on the other hand, seldom bathed and were easily detected by animals. When whites and Lenape hunted together, the Lenape were invariably more successful. As the human population increased, however, the animal population began to decrease.

Iroquois nations from the area around what is now New York had already made a conquest of the Susquehannocks along the Susquehanna River. The increasing influence of the Iroquois was at first no cause for alarm in Lenape-hocking. By the 1730s, however, the Iroquois were in Philadelphia and making treaties *for* the Lenape. The Proprietary Council, led in part by William Penn's sons John, Richard, and Thomas, thought it would be easier to deal with the Iroquois whose territory in Pennsylvania was not yet being threatened, instead of with the Lenape.

Promises were made. On October 13, 1736, James Logan, President of the Penns' Proprietary Council, addressed Iroquois leaders who were representing the Lenape. Here in modern English are paraphrased excerpts from his speech:

> *"Brethren, four years ago a great treaty was held here.... We confirmed all our former treaties with you. We brightened the Chain of Friendship. We opened and cleared the path between your country and ours, and made ourselves and you one body and one people. It was agreed that you should come down and visit us and more fully and absolutely confirm that treaty, which you did a few days ago. And it was done not only in behalf of ourselves and yourselves, but for our children and children's children, to all generations, as long as the sun, moon, and earth endure. This treaty, by which we are to become as one people, and one body, is in the strongest terms confirmed, never to be changed, but to be kept in everlasting remembrance."*

Promises. The Lenape were pleased. After all, from the time of William Penn's arrival—indeed, for thousands of years—they had proved their willingness to share Creator's land with strangers. They may have considered themselves allied with the Iroquois. Promises were sacred. Trust prevailed. There would be enough for everybody.

Promises were a very important expression of Lenape spirituality. Promises were made with a good heart, and were not to be forgotten or discarded. The Lenape believed promises were a spiritual power that helps to hold families, villages, and civilizations together. Promises should never be made lightly. Both the Iroquois and the Lenape knew promises should come from a good heart. We know that, too.

There are promises we make to ourselves. Promises to family and relatives. Promises to friends, community, and country. Some make promises that are spiritual commitments. Others make promises that are building blocks for strong commercial relationships. Employers make promises to employees and employees make promises to employers. Corporations make promises regarding the honesty and integrity of their business. Nations make promises with other nations. There are promises made to Planet Earth. Without promises there can be no cohesion, no successful enterprise, and no civilization. Every promise is made before the all-seeing eye of Creator, and the way we keep our promises reveals the nature of our spirituality.

But dark shadows were already entering Lenape-hocking. Indians did not know, for example, that European civilization had been exposed to alcohol for several thousand years, and many of its people were still being subdued by it. Without those years of experience Indians had no more defenses to counteract the disease of alcoholism than they had to counteract the White Man's disease of smallpox.

In 1683, William Penn wrote about Indians to the Committee of the Free Society of Traders in London:

> *Since the Europeans came into these parts, they are grown great lovers of strong liquors.... If they are heated with liquors, they are restless till they have enough to sleep; that is their cry, Some more, and I will go to sleep.*

People in danger of losing their land and livelihood became vulnerable to alcohol-induced sleep. This was a potent but treacherous escape from reality into temporary forgetfulness. There is no way to avoid reality but to face it. Trying to avoid reality makes people vulnerable to exploitation. The sons of William Penn had no intention of keeping their promises. They did not care that spirituality and keeping promises are linked together. But keeping promises is an indication of one's spirituality.

CHAPTER 23

THE SMILES OF GREED

Among the microfilmed documents of Thomas, Richard, and John Penn from 1762, are the minutes of a meeting with Lenape leaders dated twenty-five years before on August 24, 1737. Contained therein is the incriminating evidence of the fraud the Penn brothers, sons of the honorable William Penn, perpetrated upon trusting Lenape Indians. (The English referred to them as "Delaware" Indians.)

By the summer of 1737, the Penn brothers had inherited their father's debts. They needed to acquire land that could be sold at a profit to immigrants. Their troubles began a few years before when William Penn's grandson, also named William, inherited 10,000 acres of land from his grandfather. The original intent was to place this land "in some proper and beneficial places in this Province by his trustees...." According to previous treaties this would have been land *already purchased* from the Indians.

The story continues as it was carefully researched twenty-one years later by Charles Thomson and published in London in 1759:

> *William Allen ... was selling the land in the Minisinks which had never been purchased of the Indians...."* (This included the area in present-day Monroe County near Delaware Water Gap. It was inhabited by Shawanese Indians and was part of the Munsey-Lenape nation. Neither William Penn nor any Indians had authorized purchase of large amounts of land this far to the north, especially because it belonged to an independent nation.) *These 10,000 acres Mr. Allen purchased of William Penn the grandson, and by virtue of a warrant or order of the trustees to Jacob Taylor, surveyor-general, to survey the said 10,000 acres, he had part of that land located or laid out in the Minisinks, because it was good land.... Had he contented himself with securing the right, and suffered the lands to remain in the possession of the Indians till it had been duly purchased and paid for, no ill consequences would have ensued.*

Shawanese and Munsey Indians who lived there had sold nothing and began to protest. The Penns devised a plan of keeping William Allen's money and simultaneously paying off the Indians. A lottery was quickly established, where winning ticket-holders would get land, Indians would be paid from the profits, and everyone would be happy. Not enough people bought tickets, however, and soon ticket-holders as well as Munsey and Shawanese Indians were complaining.

And so the scheme of the "Walking Purchase" was hatched. A "lost" deed from 1686 was produced by Colonial authorities. The deed stated William Penn had paid for land along the Delaware River beginning at a point near present-day Wrightstown, Delaware and continuing back as far as a man could walk in a day and a half. Two elderly men were also presented, Joseph Wood and William Biles, who claimed they had seen William Penn give a few trinkets to some Indians who had signed a document, but they had never actually read the contents of the document. Now was the time, said the Penns, for that land to be walked and surveyed.

The Lenape chiefs, Nutimus, Lappawinzoe, Monokyhickan, and Tishekunk, had no opportunity to receive legal advice. They were honest and honorable men who the Penns welcomed with warm smiles. Minutes of the meeting on August 24, 1737, reported that the Penns were "pleased to see them, and [were] always glad of such opportunities to renew the old League and Friendship that had been established with them." But their smiles were treacherous. Hidden in those smiles was greed and unconscionable manipulation.

An interpreter who went by the colorful name of Barefoot Brinston (also Brunsden or Brunston) was presented. The Indians were told about the "lost" deed and the newly-found "copy" that replaced it. "They are sufficiently convinced of the truth whereof," said the meeting's minutes.

The Lenape spokesman was recorded as saying that "as the Indians and white people had always lived together in good understanding, they (the Indians) requested they be permitted to remain on their present settlements and plantations, even within the purchase, without being molested." The minutes then state, "In answer to which the assurances that were given at Pennsbury were repeated and confirmed to them, and the Proprietor told them he would speak further to them to-morrow."

To the Indians a verbal promise was as solid as rock and just as permanent. Reassured by the promises made on August 24, fifteen Lenape Indians signed with their marks an altogether different document on the following day. There is no indication that any interpreter was present *that* day to warn the Indians of the treacherous changes that had been made!

> *We ... do, for ourselves and all other the Delaware (Lenape) Indians fully, clearly, and absolutely remise, release, and for ever quit claim unto the said John Penn, Thomas Penn, and Richard*

Penn, all our right, title, interest, and pretensions whatsoever of, in, or to the said tract or tracts of land and every part and parcel thereof, so that neither we, or any of us, or our children shall or may at any time hereafter, have challenge, claim, or demand any right, title, interest, or pretensions whatever of, in, or to the said tract or tracts of land, or any part thereof, but of and from the same shall be excluded, and forever debarred."

Some smiles are honest. Others are not. Beware of friendly smiles motivated by greed. Investigate what you're told. Confer with trusted and knowledgeable acquaintances. Don't act hastily, or let down your guard. Learning to discern is an important goal in the spiritual life.

CHAPTER 24

RESPECT

I admire the Lenape people who lived long ago near the waters of Martin's Creek, north of present-day Easton, Pennsylvania. I admire them because of the respect they gave to someone with differing opinions, even though those opinions were detrimental to their own traditions.

In 1737, the infamous "Walking Purchase" (part of the Penns' fraudulent land grab) had altered their lives. Their village was within the new boundaries, and they grew progressively more insecure.

We now turn to the year 1744. A young missionary named David Brainerd crossed the Delaware River and entered the wilderness that in a few years would become the town of Easton. He traveled northward and built a cabin for himself at what is now the village of Martin's Creek, Pennsylvania. Plagued by many ailments that made even horseback riding very painful—including consumption that would take his life in only three years—he soon gained the respect of the villagers because he was strong despite his weakness. On Sunday June 24, 1744, he wrote in his journal: "Extremely feeble; scarce able to walk: however, visited my Indians and took much pains to instruct them; laboured with some that were much disaffected to Christianity."

Disaffected? Small wonder. The Lenape villagers had never heard of the Ten Commandments, but they were finding people who called themselves Christians with a notable disregard for the last of those Commandments: "You shall not covet anything that is your neighbor's." The covetousness for Indian land was encroaching everywhere.

The Lenape were bravely and desperately trying to cling to their beloved traditions. David Brainerd made little or no effort to learn what might be of value in their ancient heritage. To him, the wilderness was a place where demons lurked, and those who lived there were undoubtedly living with demons. The Indians knew the good qualities of wolves, and did not understand the European farmers' perception of wolves as killers of farm animals. David Brainerd was dismayed when the Indians joyously imitated the howling of wolves during happy celebrations held in the face of increasing insecurity.

On July 21, 1744, he wrote in his journal:

> *Towards night in my burden respecting my work among the Indians began to increase much; and was aggravated by hearing ... that they intended to meet together the next day for an idolatrous feast and dance.... I knew that they were met together to worship devils, and not God; and this made me cry earnestly, that God would now appear, and help me in my attempts to*

break up this idolatrous meeting.

The next day he laboriously rode to the Lenape village. That night he wrote in his journal: *When I came to them, I found them engaged in their frolic; but through divine goodness I persuaded them to desist and attend to my preaching.*

What impresses me more than David Brainerd's dogged determination is the respect he received from those Lenape Indians. They were helpless to change the probability of losing their homes, their beloved mountains, the beautiful creek, and the sacred river that flowed just beyond. Helplessness in the face of insecurity and adversity can breed not only anxiety but anger.

They may have tried to ignore what was happening all around them, but they could not escape the lingering, fearsome abyss of the unknown. Nevertheless, they rejected anger, setting aside their anxieties. They celebrated their heritage with the dances, joyous shouts, and slow, steady heartbeat-like drumming their ancestors had cherished. And then David Brainerd came and told them that almost everything they had learned from their beloved ancestors was the product of an evil spirit, and should be discarded as less than worthless.

The Lenape could have reacted in nasty ways. They could have said: "Who are you, stranger, who needs an interpreter because you won't learn our language? Who do you think you are, coming from those who take our land, kill the animals we need for food, cut down trees Creator made in abundance to help swallow downpours of water, and then tell us we are only ignorant heathen savages?"

They could have said all of that and more, *but they didn't.*

They did not respond in anger or disrespect. They never threatened Brainerd, but gave him safe passage wherever he went. Would *we* have been so kind? The white man's world was opinionated and dogmatic. Too many Christians were convinced of their own monopoly on divine truth. Too many people would argue but few would *listen* enough to learn anything beyond their own immediate horizons.

The Lenape were unique. They were judged by crimes committed ten years later by a few young men who went out of control. The long years of patience were too easily forgotten. But those Lenape who lived along Martin's Creek near the Delaware River, like most of the Lenape, respected even those who despised their Lenape traditions.

I admire them.

It is not wrong to look beyond the tight little box of one's own opinions. It is not wrong to examine and evaluate other opinions. Unexamined dogmatism can breed ignorance. Ignorance can breed intolerance. And how can this be conducive to thoughtful spirituality? Respect acknowledges diversity. Respectfulness is not rude. It does not put people down by indulging in name-calling. Respect means we do not insist everyone must think and be like us.

Respect was the Lenape way. It is still a good way to follow.

CHAPTER 25

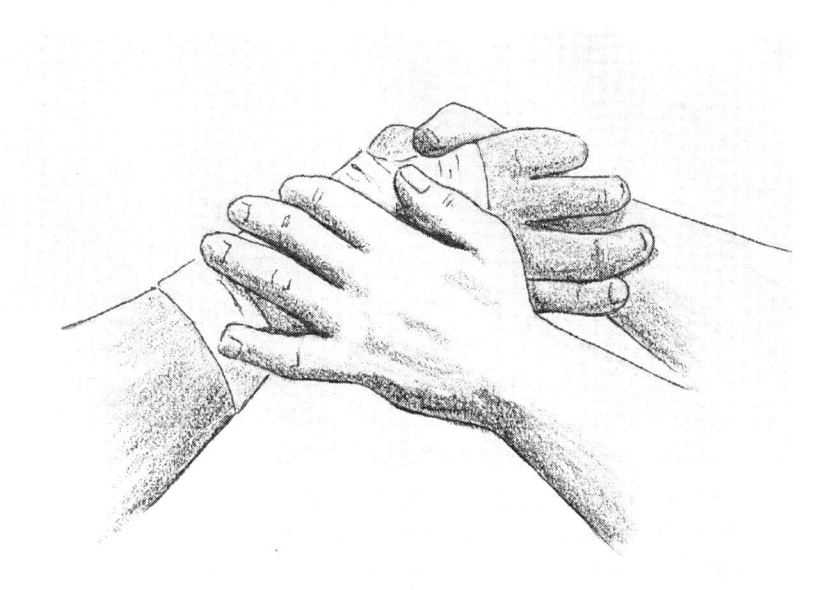

EGOTISM – AND COMPASSION

July, 1755: England was at war with France. Major-General Edward Braddock led an army to attack the French at Fort Duquesne (now Pittsburgh). As they crossed the Monongahela River, however, they encountered a French and Indian ambush. Refusing to accept advice from George Washington, his then *aide-de-camp*, to not fight in the European style of straight battle lines and meeting the enemy face-to-face, Braddock's army was torn to shreds. Braddock was wounded and died four days later.

His character was described by William Allen in a letter written from Philadelphia dated July 24, 1755. William Allen, you'll remember, was the land speculator who, twenty years before, purchased 10,000 acres in Munsey-Lenape territory from the Penns—lands they had no right to sell. He was also chief justice of colonial Pennsylvania and a businessman with international contacts. He wrote:

> *The [recent] defeat of the King's forces has put every thing in the greatest confusion.... General Braddock ... was attacked by one third of his number ... one half of his party either killed or wounded.... The general ... was ... obstinate and self-sufficient, above taking advice, and laughed to scorn all [who told him] that war in our Wood Country was to be carried on in a different manner from that in Europe.*

Egotism. Braddock refused to open his mind to important new ideas. He was of upper-class English society and he flaunted it. But pretentiousness meant little to the Lenape. They enjoyed a classless society. Titles meant little. They would not be impressed by the number of academic degrees a person held or how much income someone had. Along with other northeastern woodland people they believed merit is more important than heredity, and service to the community more important than social or economic status. They were renowned for rhetorical ability, but nevertheless convinced that wisdom and spirituality are more important than charismatic crowd-arousing speeches. They were respectful, however, and kept their personal opinions to themselves.

Egotists frequently boost themselves by demeaning others, but low self-esteem is foreign to Lenape wisdom and spirituality. When praying, for example, traditional Lenape raise their heads instead of bowing or kneeling. It's not disrespectful. Quite the contrary. It's a grateful acknowledgment that although we may be flawed human beings, Creator is willing to visit us and invite us to stand tall. Lenape traditions even describe Creator meeting with animals of the forest and holding council with them. There is a healthy balance between egotism and low self-esteem.

Compassion also belongs in Lenape wisdom and spirituality. Terrible things happen in wartime. Not even the best-trained army can boast of being immune from the possibility of committing atrocities. But the Moravian missionary, Christian Frederick Post, made an interesting entry in his journal dated August 29, 1758. Although Shingas, a renowned Lenape war chief in western Pennsylvania, was fighting against the English, Mr. Post felt safe and comfortable dining with him:

> *I dined with Shingas; he told me, though the English had set a great price on his head, he had never thought to revenge himself, but was always very kind to any prisoners that were brought in; and that ... he would do all in his power to bring about an established peace, and wished he could be certain of the English being in earnest.*

Three years before, a prisoner of Shingas named Charles Stuart had made this journal entry for Wednesday November 2, 1755:

> *"We marched off for Allegheney Mountain, having now King Shingas, Captain Jacobs, Captain Will, and Captain John Peter (names of Indian chiefs) with their respective parties along with us.... The Indians held a council where we afterwards understood they had determined to put John Condon and myself to death. The deaths we were to suffer were as follows. First our fingers were to be cut off and we were to be forced to eat them. Then our eyes pulled out, which we were also to eat. After which we were to be put on a scaffold and burned.... After the council in general had agreed to put us to this death, and waited only for Shingas as chief judge to give his consent, he rose up from his seat and objected against it, saying of me that when I was hurt he was hurt himself; [and] if I died he would die too, adding that [he] had lived on the frontiers and people had frequently called at [his] house ... and [he] had always been supplied with provisions...."*

One man's experience of receiving compassion was not forgotten. Mr. Stuart continued:

> *Rising up from his seat with appearance of deep concern on his countenance he addressed his prisoners with great solemnity, telling them that he was sorry for what had happened between*

them and the English, but that the English and not the Indians were the cause of the present war. He then proceeded to give account of those causes and said that he with five other chiefs ... had applied to General Braddock and enquired what he intended to do with the land if he could drive the French and their Indians away. To which General Braddock replied that the English [would] inhabit and inherit the land. On which Shingas asked General Braddock whether the Indians that were friends to the English might not be permitted to live and trade among the English and have hunting ground sufficient to support themselves and families.... On which General Braddock said that no savage should inherit the land.

Major-General Braddock, with too much egotism and not nearly enough compassion, drove the Lenape into supporting the French. Shingas, the Lenape warrior, exemplifies the wisdom and spiritual qualities that Major-General Braddock never had. Shingas did not lose those qualities even in time of bitter warfare. Can we do as well when our own spirit and character are being tested?

FALL BACK TO OLLI Member Social

Friday, October 26, 2018
12:30 – 3:00 p.m.
Compton Park Community Center
16101 Compton Dr., Tampa, FL 33647

Join us for a FREE, enjoyable afternoon as we celebrate OLLI's 25th anniversary throughout the year.

Plenty of free parking, and a *complimentary luncheon* provided by OLLI at the beautiful Compton Park Community Center in Tampa Palms.

RSVPs are essential for this catered event.

Please let us know you plan to attend by calling **813-974-8036** or emailing **ollivol@gmail.com** any time before Oct. 22.

CHAPTER 26

> WANISHI

GRATITUDE

The most frequently used word in the Lenape language is *Wanishi* (pronounced wah-NEE-she). It means "Thank you." Those who follow traditional Lenape spirituality wake up with it on their hearts, and it will be among their last thoughts as they go to sleep. In times of crisis, *Wanishi* expresses gratitude to Creator for being gifted with enough strength to get through the night and through the day. If tragedy strikes, *Wanishi* is expressed as gratitude for the good memories that linger.

In human relationships, as well as in a relationship with Creator, *Wanishi* is spoken in gratitude for common tasks within the home, little and big favors, and acts of kindness no matter how great or small. The list goes on and on. A traditional Lenape may ponder and ask why Thanksgiving Day in America is only one day in a year, when *every* day is intended for giving thanks.

A Lenape who understands traditional spirituality may also wonder why people fill their prayers with lists of needs. Does Creator lack knowledge so it is necessary to be told of those needs? Isn't it better to fill one's prayers with gratitude for what we *already* have?

The same Lenape may wonder why *many* people are asked to pray for someone who is ill or has a need. Does Creator count the requests before deciding to act? It could be said that prayer support from many people is a helpful reminder of friends providing the goodwill and spiritual energy that encourages strength and gratitude. A person well acquainted with Lenape spirituality might suggest it would be more helpful if people expressed thoughtful kindness *directly to* the individual in need.

Regarding gratitude, another question might be raised: "Does Creator really need a pat on the back?" No. By expressing gratitude, a person fills his or her own heart with the positive energy Creator will use for a good purpose.

When Major-General Braddock was leading his army toward Fort Duquesne against the French, two people from opposite sides would begin a friendship in the heat of battle that would produce gratitude from one generation to another.

The first was a young man named William Henry, one of several gunsmiths in Lancaster, Pennsylvania. One hundred fifty years later, on May 16, 1906, a descendant of his, John Woolf Jordan of Philadelphia, wrote to his cousin Granville Henry in Nazareth, Pennsylvania, that he had found William Henry's handwritten autobiography. In it, William Henry stated he was hired as a "contracting armourer," not a soldier. This is why, wrote Mr. Jordan, their ancestor's name did not appear in Braddock's Army muster roll. William Henry's job was to repair defective guns for the British Army.

The second was a young Lenape warrior named Killbuck (or, in the Lenape language, *Gelelemend*), born in 1737, in a village at Lehigh Gap near present-day Palmerton, Pennsylvania. His family was forced to move westward while he was still a child. He was barely eighteen years old when he heard Major-General Braddock's boast that the English would push all Indians out of western Pennsylvania, which was enough to cause him and his people to help the French in the French and Indian War.

During the battle where Braddock's army was ripped to shreds, young Killbuck was wounded and about to be dispatched by British bayonets, when William Henry risked his own life to save Killbuck. In a show of gratitude, Killbuck suggested an exchange of names—something considered a great honor by Indians. William Henry of Lancaster had no desire to take an Indian name, but he permitted Killbuck to take his.

One of Killbuck's descendants, Phyllis Donovan (now living in Vermont), writes:

> *Because Indians did not own property their name was the most precious gift they could bestow on someone else. It alone was his. They thought that it was the one thing that truly belonged to them, along with their visions, dreams, and songs.*

Forty-five years after the battle, one of William Henry's sons was traveling through Pennsylvania and Ohio. On December 10, 1800, he wrote to his brother:

> *I visited old William Henry (referring to Killbuck, who was then sixty-three years old), who expressed the highest satisfaction at seeing me. I presented him with blankets.... He returned his thanks to me in his native language.... The old man speaks very good English but his heart was so full that he could not give utterance to gratitude but in his native language...*

Furthermore, in 1863, more than a hundred years after William Henry of Lancaster rescued Killbuck, an aging grandson of William Henry of Lancaster, William Henry III, wrote of a visit his father had once received from Killbuck in 1774 (Killbuck was revisiting places of his early life in Pennsylvania, and had stopped in Lancaster to see William Henry, who was, unfortunately, in Philadelphia at that time):

> *[Killbuck] told my father ... 'Say to your father, Indian never forgets,' and ... on the battlefield he had changed family names, as the greatest honor he could confer. He and his children should ever gratefully remember the family 'Henry' and they might always feel a guarantee of safety among their tribes.*

To this day, there are Killbuck descendants who carry the name "Henry," usually as a middle name.

Wanishi. Gratitude. There are all kinds of experiences to be thankful for, especially the life-changing ones. *Wanishi* is the most important word in the Lenape language and, when it comes from the heart, deserves to be the most important word in any language.

CHAPTER 27

WHEN CRISIS COMES

A crisis often brings out the best or the worst in people, as occurred when the war between England and France intruded into northeastern Pennsylvania. The years after the Walking Purchase were tense, and displacement of the Lenape (now better known as Delawares) and Shawanee accelerated. Some moved into the Wyoming Valley (where Wilkes-Barre is now located) in the Pennsylvania mountains. Others went to western Pennsylvania, eastern Ohio, Kansas, Oklahoma, Wisconsin, Canada, and elsewhere.

Attempting to soften up the frontier for an invasion, the French went far and wide hiring warriors and assigning them the grisly task of making surprise attacks on settlers living in vulnerable locations.

On August 28, 1758, Christian Frederick Post (a missionary from the Moravian Church) described in his journal a conversation with an Indian on the western Pennsylvania frontier. The Indian said: "Did you not see the woman lying in the road that was killed by the Indians, that the English hired?" Mr. Post replied: "Brother, do consider how many thousand Indians the *French* have hired to kill the English, and how many they have killed along the frontiers." Post knew it was important to understand both sides of a story.

In Lenape-hocking one crisis followed another. In April 1755, Charles Broadhead, who lived in the vicinity of present-day Stroudsburg, Pennsylvania, rode up to the Wyoming Valley and, *without evidence or authority*, charged the native people with the French-instigated murderous raids occurring in present-day Berks County. Teedyuscung, the Indian chief in that area, denied the accusations. Broadhead then demanded the Indians leave "his" land, and said "the English were preparing to take a severe revenge" against them. Broadhead had no evidence of this, either. He was not willing to gather all the facts. The land in question was part of the territory seized by the Walking Puchase of 1737.

Teedyuscung asked Broadhead to carry a message from the Indians to the Governor of Pennsylvania, assuring him they did not want to break the Chain of Friendship, and to bring back the Governor's answer. Months passed, but there was no reply. Broadhead never went to Philadelphia. He had refused to make the extra effort for a mission of peace, a mistake that had tragic consequences.

By late November, believing the threats to Lenape-hocking to be real, the Lenape began hostilities by attacking settlements along the east side of the Lehigh. A number of settlers were killed or driven out.

Before the winter of 1755-56 was over, however, the series of raids had ceased. Teedyuscung agreed to meet Pennsylvania Government representatives at Easton, where the Lehigh and Delaware Rivers join. Consternation erupted when Teedyuscung arrived for treaty negotiations wearing colorful French clothing, making it obvious he could easily join with the French.

During a series of peace talks, Teedyuscung accused the Penns of fraud. A truce was adopted to allow time for an investigation. Sir William Johnson, the British commissioner of Northern Indian Affairs, was consulted.

William Johnson, realizing he could not do everything, appointed George Croghan, a colonial trader, to investigate the charges. Mr. Croghan's appointment read,

> *By nature of the power and authority to me given by his Majesty, I do authorize you ... to call a meeting of the Shawanese and Delawares ... [to] hear their complaints, and endeavour all in your power to have justice done to them....*

Yes, there was confrontation—but no hasty decisions. There was also consultation with a neutral person, and delegation of responsibility. It was a good process.

The Quakers (also known as the Friendly Association), a prominent Christian group in Philadelphia, had made careful inquiries about Teedyuscung's charge and were satisfied of his truthfulness. In July, 1757, their trustees and treasurer wrote a lengthy letter to the Pennsylvania governor:

> *...a considerable number of us thought it necessary to enter into a subscription towards raising a fund to supply the deficiency of what ought in justice to be contributed by the Proprietaries on this occasion; and a considerable sum was immediately subscribed....*

Pennsylvania's colonial leaders were furious. At this point, reimbursing the Indians for land seized in 1737 would have been an admission of guilt. The Quakers were right, but their generous offer was rejected.

In the end, through some daring manipulation, the colonial government managed to deceive Teedyuscung and peace was restored. It was a temporary peace, however, as deception perpetuated tragedy.

At least some people made an honest attempt for justice to prevail. Teedyuscung and his people in the Wyoming Valley had genuinely wanted to restore the Chain of Friendship. A military solution had not been necessary.

Trying to do one's best in a time of crisis is not always rewarded as one would hope. Fairness and justice, with a willingness to make sacrifices, is the wisest way to a durable peace. Times of personal, national, or international crisis can be an opportunity to bring out the best in ourselves. This is very relevant for understanding the meaning of spirituality. It's a big mistake to think spirituality consists only of folding one's hands in prayer. Spirituality includes not only the way we pray but what we do with our life, how we do it, and why we do it.

CHAPTER 28

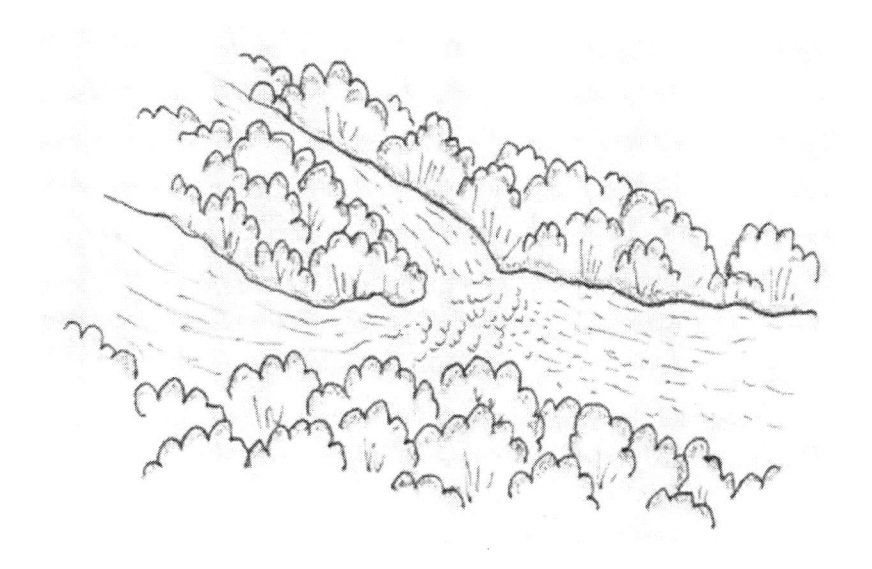

ALLIANCE OF THE WATERS

The Lehigh and Delaware Rivers join between Easton, Pennsylvania and Phillipsburg, New Jersey to form an alliance that strengthens them both. From that point they are inseparable, flowing together as long as the sun shines upon their waters and the mountains guide their path.

Two hundred fifty years ago colonists regarded the Lehigh River as a branch of the Delaware, actually calling it the "west branch of the Delaware." The main branch became the boundary between colonies.

The Lenape regarded it differently. The rivers were not boundaries, but thoroughfares of communication. Bringing diverse people together was one of the contributions the Lenape gave to their long-ago world. Although they could meet in various locations, they cherished the place where the waters came together. Representatives of many different tribes met with the *Grandfathers*—the title by which the Lenape were known—to try and resolve disagreements without bloodshed and tears. They would sit on the grass and listen respectfully not only to each other, but to the never-ending music of the Lehigh and Delaware Rivers coming together: splashing roughly at first, then moving quietly southward to help replenish the Great Ocean.

Unlike the European practice, reports were never written about the topics of those ancient negotiations in Lenape-hocking. Successful diplomacy that prevents violence, however, is a victory for humanity. It requires special skills, and is best achieved by those on all sides of a problem who have a profound wisdom and spirituality sensitive to the legitimate needs of others. Successful diplomacy also requires honesty. These were qualities the Lenape cherished.

While two other rivers, the Schuylkill and the Delaware, provided easy access to the west and east of Philadelphia—the seat of the Provincial government—treaty meetings took place in Easton, which was then a scrubby, recently-settled frontier village. It was there the Alliance of the Waters could be seen and heard as a reminder that unity *could* come from diversity.

It doesn't require much imagination to perceive the Lenape wanted the colonial government to appreciate the Alliance of the Waters. It was a gift from Creator. It united for the good of all those who needed its cool, clear water, whether they were humans, animals, or vegetation nourished by the water.

Trees along the river banks helped control floods. The Lenape called them "tree people," guardians of the environment. Trees swallowed great amounts of rainwater that otherwise would have caused flooding. The Lenape did not know the scientific reason for the pure air they breathed, but their exhaled carbon dioxide nourished the vegetation which then provided clean oxygen. The Lenape knew in their hearts that ruthlessly cutting down trees diminished the balance their Creator had given to the earth. Appreciating the value of Creator's gifts also reveals a person's spirituality.

In the 1750s, the French and English brought war to the world of the Lenape and dragged them into its deadly embrace. The French called the English "land-grabbers," and the English declared the French cheated the Indians in trade. As in every war, there was bloodshed and innocent people died.

Lenape leaders desired to re-establish the chain of friendship. The terrible excesses of young warriors at war were brought back under the control of elders, grandmothers, and village chiefs. Discussions to resolve problems made it necessary for everything to be brought into the open. This was no problem as traditionally the Lenape found it acceptable to discuss anything. No subject was out of bounds, regardless of how awful a topic might seem.

Disagreement *could* be expressed, but always calmly, respectfully, and without resorting to name-calling. All were expected to hear different opinions patiently and without rancor. Those who did not control themselves, the volume of their voices, or the language they used, were considered unworthy of respect. Silence would be given to opinionated people. Aggressively opinionated persons would find themselves ignored and shunned.

The alliance of the waters: two beautiful rivers uniting. When human beings find a way to join amicably together in harmony with the natural environment—even if it requires sacrifices—it is an expression of genuine spirituality.

The sacred Lehigh and Delaware Rivers continue to unite. The music of the waters made an important contribution for resolving problems. If we could but look and listen, we might learn what the Lenape of many generations ago knew in their hearts. It is better to join together and help each other than to pursue a separate, solitary life concerned only with our own path and our own self-interest.

This is wisdom. This is spirituality.

CHAPTER 29

SHINGAS WEEPS

November, 1758: the French and British were still at war, both on the European Continent and in America. Northeastern woodland people were caught in the middle. In Easton, Teedyuscung had just signed a peace treaty with the English governor. The news was carried quickly to Indians who had migrated westward in hope of finding peace from the white man's scrambling, dusty, dirty frontier settlements.

While researching microfilms of old documents from this time period, I found a copy of a speech by the English General John Forbes to the Shawanese and Delawares in the mountains of western

Pennsylvania, followed by a similar speech to King Beaver (Delaware chief also called Tamaqui or Amockwi) and Shingas (Delaware chief and brother to King Beaver). After informing the Shawanese and Delawares of the peace treaty, General Forbes urged them: *Let the French fight their own battles.* He wanted to stop them from supporting a French invasion that threatened to take over western Pennsylvania.

Turning to King Beaver and Shingas, he began with the usual form of address: *Brethren, King Beaver and Shingas, and all the Warriors who join with you.* Then he asked them, as the leaders of their people, to not support the French. The record of that meeting continues:

> ...Shingas rose up and said, "...We shall think of it and take it into due consideration; and when we have considered it well, then we will ... send it to all the towns and nations as you desired us.

A good response for any decision-making! *When we have considered it...* this made it a group decision. *When we have considered it* well... required careful examination and evaluation by all who were part of the decision-making.

We know Shingas was a courageous, powerful, and highly respected man. Could someone like Shingas ever break down and cry?

Several years ago I searched online for the Dauphin County Library in Harrisburg, Pennsylvania, wondering what it might have for my Lenape research. My computer, however, misled me by giving directions that sent me to a small branch library on Front and Walnut Streets. I was disappointed. "Well," I said to myself, "I might as well go in, although I'm probably wasting my time." But it was there that I found a valuable book by Edwin MacMinn. It was published in 1900 in a limited edition of only 1,000 copies under the title, *On the Frontier With Colonel Antes.* Embedded in Chapter 17 is an eyewitness account of the death and burial of Shingas' wife in 1762.

The unnamed eyewitness also included some observations of Lenape attempts at healing:

> *[After] convincing his patient that his disorder is such that no common physician has it in his power to relieve, [the doctor] will next endeavor to convince him of the necessity of making him very strong....*

Strengthening the spirit of a person was an important aspect of spiritual healing among the Lenape and other Native American nations.

The witness then described the death and burial of Shingas' wife:

> *I was present in the year 1762, at the funeral of a woman of the highest rank and respectability, the wife of the valiant Delaware chief Shingask (sic); at the moment that she died her death was announced through the village by women especially appointed for that purpose, who went through the streets crying, 'She is no more! She is no more!' The place on a sudden exhibited a scene of universal mourning....*

According to Lenape tradition her name would not have been spoken, lest her spirit be called back because it was interrupted on its journey into the next world. The eyewitness then described the graveside scene:

> *The [mourners] formed themselves into a kind of [semi-circle] on the south side of the grave, and seated themselves on the ground, while the disconsolate husband retired by himself to a spot at some distance, where he was seen weeping with his head bowed to the ground. ... In this situation we remained for more than two hours; not a sound was heard from any quarter, though the numbers that attended were very great; nor did any person move from his seat to view the body, which had been lightly covered over with a clean white sheet. Sighs and sobs were now and then heard from the female mourners, so uttered as not to disturb the assembly....*

From this story, I have learned four important lessons about Lenape insights into spirituality and strength of character:

After doing one's best it is important to be strong and accept what cannot be changed.

Support from friends is essential.

Silence can be more helpful than verbal clichés. Words cannot replace being quietly there.

And to the question, "Can strong people cry?" the answer is a definitive "Yes." There are times to allow emotions to surface. There are times when it's okay for even the strongest to cry.

Shingas was a strong and courageous man. Instead of becoming angry and cursing the sickness that caused his beloved wife's death, he showed his humanity—indeed, his manliness—and allowed himself to cry.

The women, too, were strong. They *had* to be in those times. But they also wept. For women and men alike it is okay and *healthy* to cry in times of genuine distress. Don't be ashamed when tears come sincerely to your eyes. Lenape spirituality respected inner strength, self-control, courage—and tears.

CHAPTER 30

COURAGE

Courage was high on the list of every American native nation. Courage was also held in high regard by immigrants. In fact, courage has been—and continues to be—valued throughout the entire world. It is something that rises from the heart of a person. If used in a good way it can be an expression of a person's spirituality.

An example of courage might be found in the ancient custom of "running the gauntlet." Sometimes this took place in the northeastern woodlands, especially by the Iroquois. But the origins of "running the gauntlet" may be found in ancient Rome where it was a method of execution. A prisoner was forced to run between two rows of men armed with clubs. If he survived he could be forced to run again until he died. Later in European history if he succeeded in running the distance he might be allowed to live. In the English navy, whips similar to the harsh "cat o' nine tails" were used. A man's bare back might receive a dozen lashes before the run began so the run itself would be even more painful.

In Iroquois territory, "running the gauntlet" has been traced as far back as 1641. The most detailed description I have found comes from Moses Van Campen, a prisoner of the Iroquois in 1781 (during the American War for Independence). Van Campen told the story to his grandson, J. Niles Hubbard, who wrote his biography. It tells of personal courage, and the admiration courage was held with by Native Americans. The incident took place at an Iroquois village named Caneadea along the Genesee River south of Rochester, New York. It's worth quoting at length. I've substituted the word "women" instead of the objectionable word "squaw," which can have a demeaning connotation:

> ...it was not always a scene of cruelty, but was often made the source of high amusement to the Indians, without causing any great suffering to the captive. Much of [the captive's] success depended upon the manner in which the prisoner conducted himself before the warriors. Should he present a fearless, independent spirit, it might perhaps win for him the admiration of his captors, and they would allow him to pass unharmed. But should he appear cowardly and timid, he would be most surely treated with the utmost severity....
>
> The Indian ladies were furnished with long whips, and as they stood lightly tapping them on the ground, it was certain that they were designing to use them.... The warriors took no active part, but remained spectators of the scene, while the villagers formed themselves on the sides....
>
> While Van Campen was standing in front of his men, he amused himself by observing ... his fellow prisoners straightening their muscles and nerving themselves for a vigorous effort....
>
> Just before the word was given, Van Campen saw two young [women], who appeared to have been left behind, coming along from the village very leisurely, to join the sport. They ... stood still with their whips raised, and awaited the coming of the prisoners. Presently the word 'joggo' was given, and the captives sprang forward to the race. ... Van Campen had not yet received a single blow, and was drawing near, in his rapid flight, to the two young

THE COMMON SENSE LIFE

[women] who had their whips raised, ready to strike....

Just before he reached them, the thought struck him, and as quick as lightning he gave a spring, and raised his feet, which hit them ... and sent them, as if by a whirlwind, in the same direction in which he was running. They all came down together, tumbling heels over head, and Van Campen found himself between the two [women], who were kicking and squabbling about, endeavoring to gain a more favorable position, yet he did not wait to help the ladies up, but sprang upon his feet, and made good his race.

The warriors who were spectators of this scene beheld it with the utmost delight. ...When they saw him spring and take them along with him, and as they beheld them all thrown together in a heap, they were filled with merriment and made the air ring with shouts of laughter. Some threw themselves upon the ground, and rolled and laughed, as though they were ready to burst, and long and loud was their enjoyment of this little maneuver. The prisoners by means of this diversion had all of them an easy race, arriving safely at the end of their course.

Immediately after, several of the young warriors, who were exceedingly diverted with the manner in which Van Campen had cleared himself, came up to him and patted him on the shoulder saying, "Shenawana"— "Cajena"—brave man—good fellow.

Courage coming from within a person's heart is an expression of strong spirituality. No one can acquire it for us. We must nourish it for ourselves. Courage does not drown itself in self-pity. It does not see itself as a victim but one who has received an opportunity to rise above anxiety, disaster, or tragedy. Fear and hysteria must be rejected. The support of one's friends is accepted, but one's own self-reliance is required. Good judgment must be carefully cultivated. Risk-taking must be carefully evaluated, as much as there is time to do so. Courage is not simply being willing to die for a good cause, courage means being willing to *live* for a good cause.

This was the Lenape way and the way of other Native nations; a way that is cultivated and nourished from within one's heart.

CHAPTER 31

THE SILENT YEARS

At last, most people in Pennsylvania thought, Indians of a variety of native nations were gone elsewhere. So it seemed. But it was not as it appeared.

Lenape civilization never had federal laws, as does the United States. The Lenape heritage was usually passed along from mother to daughter—unlike European civilization that was dominated by men, but it could also be passed from mother to son. What might be traditional in one village was not necessarily the rule elsewhere.

Lenape women helped reclaim the land for their descendants by marrying German (usually) farmers. The closer a farmer lived to the woman's traditional village the more eligible he was as a spouse.

While Lenape mothers took care of the garden, the task of teaching fell to the grandmothers. "My Lenape grandmother was born in 1883," I was told once. "Her grandmother was born in 1810 and *that* woman's grandmother was born around the middle of the 1700s. So there aren't that many steps from that time to this. My grandmothers' ancestors wanted to maintain their way of life on their own land."

The emphasis was on quietness. I've seen a doll with two opposite faces that has been passed down from one generation to another. Why two faces? One face of the doll was the "stone" face. It had no expression that could be seen by outsiders. On the other side, hidden under the doll's hair, was the expressive, true face. It carried a message to the child: Do not reveal your true identity. If children were known to be Indians, they could be teased incessantly by their peers.

One woman remembers her grandmother's advice, "The best way is to be like a bird in a bush. A little bird finds its way into the interior of a bush and as long as it keeps quiet and stays where it is, it will be safe. It will observe what is going on beyond the bush. It will hear and see everything. But those who are outside the bush aren't even aware that the bird is there."

Why all the silence about being an Indian? Events in the midwestern United States in 1879 provide one answer. At that time, any Indians caught off their reservation were subject to arrest. Chief Standing Bear and thirty others of the small, peaceful Ponca tribe decided to leave their reservation in Oklahoma to honor the dying wish of Standing Bear's son: to be buried with his ancestors at their traditional homeland in South Dakota.

Interior Secretary Schurz, in Washington, D.C. ordered them arrested for leaving the reservation. Sympathetic attorneys brought their case to the federal court in Omaha, Nebraska. Judge Elmer Dundy's graciously-intended decision was reported in the *Omaha Herald* on May 13, 1879. The judge wrote (capital letters are part of his ruling):

> *An Indian is a PERSON within the meaning of the laws of the United States, and ... Indians ... have the inalienable right to life, liberty, and the pursuit of happiness so long as they obey the laws and do not trespass on forbidden ground.*

The ruling reverberated through the entire United States. It was reported that same evening in the *Easton Daily Express*. Two days later, on May 15, *The Daily Free Press* in Easton, Pennsylvania, briefly noted that Chief Standing Bear and the Ponca with him were freed from their imprisonment. It added ominously that Judge Dundy's decision was "fraught with danger to whites and Indians alike." This same newspaper boasted it had "the largest circulation of any daily newspaper in the Lehigh Valley" (Easton, Bethlehem, Allentown, and entire surrounding area).

From a white person's point of view at that time, what would happen if Indians everywhere began exercising their right to life, liberty, and the pursuit of happiness? Would they leave *en masse* from their government-assigned reservations?

For Indians in eastern Pennsylvania, what was meant by "forbidden ground"? In 1742 the Colonial Government ruled Native American Indians should be removed from the entire area affected by the Walking Purchase of 1737 (see chapter 23). This did not change after America gained independence. People with Native American Indian heritage living in this vast area were in a quandary. Could the last clause of Judge Dundy's court decision, despite his good intentions, make precarious the situation of Indian descendants? After the treachery of Thomas Penn and the Proprietary Council deprived Native Americans of a legal right to live in these counties, were they illegal aliens living in their own homeland? Were they "trespassing on forbidden ground"? Anxiety breeds fear and fear increases anxiety. It's a terrible cycle.

I remember the childhood game, "Cowboys and Indians." The Indians were always the bad guys. What little colonial history that was taught in schools invariably told of massacres committed by Indians; but I don't remember ever having been told about the atrocities *done* to Indians.

***

If some families have a distant, almost-forgotten memory of a long-ago Indian ancestor the chances are this memory is based on fact. Otherwise it would not have been passed along. In some families the ancient traditions were not all forgotten.

The United States Government, in trying to categorize someone's degree of Native American Indian descent, defined "blood quantum" as the percentage of a person's Native Indian blood compared to the percentage of their non-Native Indian blood. This was not important to the Lenape. Lenape tradition knew of no such person as a "half-breed." If a white child, living with a Lenape family who had lost one of its own children, wished to become Lenape, the child could be adopted and become an Indian. All descendants of mixed marriages were considered Indians.

There are people even now who wish to maintain their Lenape identity. In Lenape woodland tradition they have every right to do so. The time has come not only to allow but to *encourage* people whose origins in the western hemisphere go back thousands of years to freely identify themselves. The time has come for the expressive and true face to be freed and show a great heritage going far back through prehistory. The time has come to take pride in the ancient wisdom and the ancient heritage!

***

Lenape tradition emphasizes the universal presence of the Great Spirit. A clan mother says, "The Great Spirit puts us here to learn. We learn through everything the Great Spirit has made, as well as the circumstances and experiences we have in life. Every experience has something to teach. Creator gives understanding and wisdom if one is humble enough to ask for it. My people believed that everyone is on a spiritual path. The purpose of our existence on this earth is to learn and grow. The question is, Where is your path taking you and what have you learned from past experiences?"

She continues: "The Lenape concept was to accept whatever happens in your life. Your circumstances will be different than everyone else. What you learn from your own experiences will therefore be different from others. Life is a journey and people must go by their own life's circumstances at their own pace. They don't ask 'Why would a good God let this or that happen to me?' Instead, they say that Creator has allowed something to happen because Creator wanted you to learn from it."

She adds: "During the Depression of the 1930s there was a Lenape woman and her husband whose home was like a clearing-house for relatives. This husband was acquainted with each person's needs. He concerned himself with finding jobs for those who needed employment. He saw to it that needy families received bags of food according to their needs. His Lenape wife handled the distribution of used clothing and household items to those who needed them. One of their favorite phrases was: 'If you have anything extra, give to somebody else.'"

The traditional Lenape way emphasized living within one's means and avoiding debt. "If you can't pay for it now, you don't need it now," parents instructed their children. Also, "Don't tell jokes that are put-downs and make other people feel bad." If someone is having a difficult time their attitude might be, "Calm down and try to figure out what you're supposed to be learning through this." They believed a person chose how it would be *after* this life by how they lived *in* this life.

A clan mother told me:

"My Lenape grandmother insisted that the kitchen had to be painted yellow because her favorite flower was yellow. She did not believe in blocking the light out of a house; nothing ever covered the windows. She believed that we should let the light in. My grandfather believed that to have peace and health in the home they had to have brown wooden floors like the bare ground, green walls like the tree-leaves in the forest, a pale blue ceiling like the sky, and no interior doors. He wanted the inside of his home to remind him of the outdoors.

"If you don't come to other people as an equal, you can't establish a good, healthy relationship with them. Don't look at people's clothes or education or jobs to respect them. Look at their heart.

"Within the family, or with people who were trusted, the Lenape were very sentimental. But they were convinced that emotions were not to be shown to strangers because they were private and personal, and were kept for intimate family relationships and among trusted friends.

"It was always very important to be on time, neither ahead of time nor late. Being on time was considered a sign of respect for other people. My people recognized that everybody has problems and is sometimes late. These attitudes were typically Munsey. It was the person who was habitually late who was not tolerated.

"In my home it was taught that the worst thing a growing child or young adult could do was to bring dishonor to the family by bad behavior. Every child was seen as Creator's gift to the mother's family, but the child did not belong only to the mother; the child belonged to all the relatives. Parents never screamed or hollered at their children. The children were told the way they were expected to live and there would be no arguments about it. Children were not whiners because they knew that their Lenape parents would not change their mind.

"Grandmother taught me that if you moved from one place to another you should take some small rocks from where you had lived to the new place."

Attachment to one's home was important.

***

And then there is the matter of what was called "Indian giving." If someone purchased something and, after using it for several years, no longer needed it, it would not thrown away. Instead, it would be given to someone. If ever that person no longer needed it, it would be returned to the original owner, who would have the right to either store it for future use or donate it to someone else.

Spirituality is much more than folding one's hands in pious prayer. Both wisdom and spirituality can be summed up in this simple phrase: "Living with a good heart."

Don't wait to receive a gift. Go and *be* a gift.

THE COMMON SENSE LIFE

AND NOW TO BEGIN...

There is so much more to be said. We have not considered the ceremonies, the medicine wheel, or the many sacred stories from long ago. We have not discussed the hardships of those who went in various directions to find a homeland they could call their own.

There is so much that could have been said, so much that *should* have been said. But what we have considered here is only a beginning to appreciate the immense value of an ancient and wise people whose presence is still in eastern Pennsylvania, and in many other places in North America, Canada, and wherever their descendants live.

Their skills were not in technology. Instead, their traditions focused on the wisdom and spirituality that makes being alive genuinely worthwhile. And they learned it not from books but from keen-sighted observation over thousands and thousands of years.

Lenape tradition holds that each person is unique. Genuineness is imperative. We can, however, choose the ancestors we wish to honor the most. We know some of our ancestors were wise, some not-so-wise, and some foolish. There were some who were good, some not-so-good, and perhaps some who were villains. Like them, we are who we are. We can choose to be better than we were. We can choose to be worse. Or we can choose to let whatever we are take its course. We can feel a special kinship with a genetic line that is special to us. We can even feel a kinship in our hearts to people we are not related to.

As far back in time as we can go, it appears the Lenape have always been people of independent minds. It should not be strange that those who have moved away, beyond the hills and forests of Lenapehocking, experienced their own history and cultural development. Nor should it be strange that those who refused to leave, or those who returned, also experienced their own history and cultural development. No one can live entirely like their ancestors of several hundred years ago.

For everyone there is a choice: to learn or not to learn. Lenape tradition shares the conviction that we either learn from experience or repeat the same mistakes over and over again. In this book we have endeavored to learn something helpful from the experiences of history. There are many other opportunities. Whenever we pick up a newspaper, for example, we read about mistakes that have been made. Can we learn something helpful from the mistakes of others as well as our own? If we choose to think and learn, then every day, week, month, and year creates the possibility for a new experience that makes life not a dead-end street but an open-hearted journey.

Every day is a new beginning.

Wanishi to my Lenape friends. What is written here is blessed with the encouragement of people who are friends *indeed*.
-- Donald R. Repsher

ABOUT THE AUTHOR

DONALD R. REPSHER was born in the town of Bangor, Pennsylvania, and is an alumnus of Bangor High School, Albright College in Reading, Pennsylvania with a B.S. degree in psychology, and United Theological Seminary in Dayton, Ohio, with an M.Div. degree in ministry. Following his career with United Methodist and Presbyterian congregations in Pennsylvania, New Jersey and New York State he developed a close friendship with descendants of the Lenape Indians whose homeland was in eastern Pennsylvania and New Jersey. He has published a chapter in *Native Americans in the Susquehanna River Valley, Past and Present,* edited by anthropologist David J. Minderhout (published by Bucknell University Press), titled "Blood Quantum and Lenape Tradition."

BIOGRAPHICAL INFORMATION

Robert Mexkalahiyat (Red Hawk) Ruth

Chief Bob is currently serving his second term as chief of the Lenape Nation of Pennsylvania. He is co-curator of *Fulfilling a Prophecy: The Past and Present of the Lenape in Pennsylvania* at the University of Pennsylvania Museum of Archaeology and Anthropology.

Philip "Wak'Tame" Rice

A Munsee/Lenape, was in active service in the U. S. Navy for eight years, and fourteen years in the Army Reserves. He served with the 3rd Marine Division in Vietnam as a Corpsman. He retired from Nursing in July 2008 after forty years. A genealogical researcher and historian, he is also a Native craftsperson in beading and leather work.

Carol Kuhn

Carol has always lived in northeastern Pennsylvania. "I was fortunate," she tells us, "to have two grandmothers who taught me what they knew of our Minsi (Munsee) family heritage. I hope others will enjoy reading what Don has written."

Chuck "Gentle Moon" De Mund

Chuck is the source of one of the main ideas that runs through this book. Living with a good heart, he says, is the essence of the Lenape spirit. He is also a ceremonial leader.

Pamela Repsher

Pam is a graduate of Reading High School and Kutztown University in Kutztown, Pennsylvania. She was an art educator in several school districts Pennsylvania. She illustrated a previous book on the Lenape for the Slate Heritage Society, titled "*Of Forest and River: The Lenape of the Slate Belt*" by Elinor Fehr and her husband, Donald Repsher.

BIBLIOGRAPHY

Chapter 1. Before the beginning
Lenape oral tradition.

Chapter 3. One or the other – or both/and plus?
The Saturday Review, date unknown.

Chapter 4. Discretion and valor
Hart, Robert Bushnell, editor, *American History Told by Contemporaries*, Vol. 1 (New York: The Macmillan Company, 1910).

Chapter 5. Columbus – and the most important journey
Hart, Robert Bushnell, *op. cit.*

Chapter 6. Verrazano: he didn't jump to conclusions
Hart, Robert Bushnell, *op. cit.*

Chapter 7. Natives discover Henry Hudson
Hart, Robert Bushnell, *op. cit.*

Chapter 8. Living on the back of a giant turtle
Oral tradition of the Lenape and other Native American tribes.

Chapter 9. The forest people
Hart, Robert Bushnell, *op. cit.*

Chapter 10. Wild-turkey people
Ballard, Jan, curator of the Jacobsburg Historical Society, Nazareth, Pennsylvania.

Hawthorne, Nathaniel, *The Great Stone Face*, in *The Old Man's Reader: History and Legends of Franconia Notch*, compiled and edited by John T. B. Mudge (Etna, New Hampshire: The Durand Press, 1995).
Oral tradition of the Lenape.

Savage, Tom, internet site of the Animal Sciences Department of Ohio State University.

Chapter 11. The people who knew wolves
Ballantine, Richard, and Jim Dutcher, *The Sawtooth Wolves* (Bearsville, New York: Rufus Publications, Inc., 1996).

Edwards, Rev. Jonathan, editor, and Sereno Edwards Dwight, *Memoirs of the Rev. David Brainerd* (New Haven, Connecticut: S. Converse, 1822).

Chapter 12. Who owns what?
De Vries, David Pieterszoon, *Kort Historiael Ende Journaels Aenteyckeninge*, Holland, 1655; trans. by Henry C. Murphy and revised by A. J. F. van Laer and published in Myers, Albert Cook, editor, *Narratives of Early Pennsylvania, West New Jersey, and Delaware, 1630-1707* (New York: Charles Scribner's Sons, 1912.

Chapter 13. It's so frustrating!
Johnson, Amandus, *The Swedes on the Delaware* (Philadelphia: International Printing Company, 1927.

Printz, Johan, 1644 report to Sweden, in Myers, Albert Cook, editor, *op. cit.*

Chapter 14. Wisdom within rocks
Oral tradition of the Lenape.

Chapter 15. A chain of friendship
Myers, Albert Cook, editor, *Narratives*, *op. cit.*
Myers, Albert Cook, editor, *William Penn's Own Account of the Lenni Lenape or Delaware Indians* (Wilmington, Delaware: The Middle Atlantic Press, 1937).

Chapter 16. Vision for now and always
Lancaster County Historical Society, *Historical Papers and Addresses of the Lancaster County Historical Society, Pennsylvania*, Vol. 1, 1896, pp. 117-118.

Myers, Albert Cook, *Narratives, op. cit.*

Chapter 17. Tamanend – and a civil civilization
Anonymous, *In Memory of Tammany*, in *The Book Shelf Scrap Book of Easton and Northampton County*, Vol. 1, Part 1, pages 1ff; the Easton Public Library, Easton, Pennsylvania.

Heckewelder, John, *History, Manners, and Customs of the Indian Nations Who Once Inhabited Pennsylvania and the Neighbouring States* (Philadelphia: Publication Fund of The Historical Society of Pennsylvania, 1876).

Chapter 18. Tamanend: America's Patron Saint
Janney, Samuel M., *The Life of William Penn* (Philadelphia, 1852; quoted by Robert Bushnell Hart, *op. cit.*

Chapter 19. Imagine!
Myers, Albert Cook, *Narratives, op. cit.*

Chapter 20. Lingering a little longer....
Myers, Albert Cook, *Narratives, op. cit.*

Chapter 21. More time with eye-witnesses
Myers, Albert Cook, *Narratives, op. cit.*

Chapter 22. Promises
Indian Treaties Printed by Benjamin Franklin, 1736-1762 (Philadelphia: The Historical Society of Pennsylvania, 1938).

Munsee-Lenape oral tradition.
Myers, Albert Cook, *Narratives, op. cit.*

Chapter 23. The smiles of greed
Penn Family Manuscripts: Indian affairs, 1757-1772 (microfilm 1577 in the Pennsylvania Archives, Harrisburg, Pennsylvania).

Thomson, Charles, *An Enquiry into the causes of the alienation of the Delaware and Shawanese Indians from the British interest* (London: J. Wilkie in St. Paul's Church-yard, 1759).

Chapter 24. Respect
Edwards, Rev. Jonathan, *Memoirs of the Rev. David Brainerd; Missionary to the Indians on the Borders of New-York, New-Jersey, and Pennsylvania, chiefly taken from his own diary, including his journal, now for the first time incorporated with the rest of his diary* (New-Haven, Connecticut: S. Converse, 1822).

Chapter 25. Egotism – and compassion
Allen, William, personal correspondence (Harrisburg, Pennsylvania: Pennsylvania Archives,
Microfilm 0896.

Oral traditions of the Pennsylvania Lenape.

Stuart, Charles, *The Captivity of Charles Stuart, 1755-1757*, edited by Beverly W. Bond, Jr., and Reprinted for the Society of the Colonial Wars in the State of Ohio, from the Mississippi Valley Historical Review, Vol. XIII, no. 1, June 1926).

Chapter 26. Gratitude
Jacobsburg Historical Society, Nazareth, Pennsylvania, manuscript collection.

Oral traditions of the Pennsylvania Lenape.

Chapter 27. When crisis comes
Penn family manuscripts: Indian Affairs, 1757-1772 (microfilm 1577 in the Pennsylvania Archives, Harrisburg, Pennsylvania).

Post, Christian Frederick, *Journal, 1758* (included in Charles Thomson, *op. cit.*)

Thomson, Charles, *op. cit.*

Chapter 28. Alliance of the Waters
Oral traditions of the Pennsylvania Lenape.

Schutt, Amy C., *Peoples of the River Valleys: The Odyssey of the Delaware Indians* (Philadelphia: University of Pennsylvania Press, 2007, p. 4).

Chapter 29. Shingas weeps
MacMinn, Edwin, *On the Frontier with Colonel Antes* (Camden, New Jersey: S. Chew and Sons, Printers, Front and Market Streets, 1900).

Penn family manuscripts: Indian Affairs, 1757-1772 (microfilm 1755 in the Pennsylvania Archives, Harrisburg, Pennsylvania).

Chapter 30. Courage
Hubbard, J. Niles, *Sketches of Border Adventures in the Life and Times of Major Moses Vancampen* (Fillmore, New York: John S. Minard, printer, 1893, from the 1842 edition.

Oral tradition of the Pennsylvania Lenape.

Wikipedia, the free encyclopedia (Internet http://wikipedia.org/wiki).

Chapter 31. The silent years
Easton Daily Express (newspaper), May 15, 1879.
Herald (newspaper), Omaha, Nebraska, May 13, 1879.
Oral tradition of the Pennsylvania Munsee-Lenape.
Pennsylvania Colonial Records, 1742 (Harrisburg, Pennsylvania).